Finding
the Keys

Finding the Keys

Reaching Thai Folk Buddhists with the Gospel

Peter & Waew Martyn

Finding the Keys
Published by Peter & Waew Martyn
with Castle Publishing Ltd
New Zealand

© 2022 Peter & Waew Martyn

ISBN 978-0-473-65628-7 (Softcover)
ISBN 978-0-473-65629-4 (ePUB)
ISBN 978-0-473-65630-0 (Kindle)

Editing:
Rachel Ross

Production & Typesetting:
Andrew Killick
Castle Publishing Services
www.castlepublishing.co.nz

Cover Design:
Paul Smith

Scriptures taken from
the Holy Bible, New International Version®, NIV®.
Copyright © 1973, 1978, 1984, 2011 by Biblica, Inc.™
Used by permission of Zondervan.
All rights reserved worldwide.

ALL RIGHTS RESERVED

No part of this publication may be reproduced,
stored in a retrieval system, or transmitted
in any form or by any means, electronic, mechanical,
photocopying, recording or otherwise,
without prior written permission from the authors.

Foreword

Peter and Waew Martyn met in Northeast Thailand in 1991 while Peter was in the region working on a Thai Government dairy farming development project. After marrying, they returned to New Zealand in 1993, where they settled and started a family. Twelve years later, God called them back to Northeast Thailand as missionaries. Over the next 13 years, Peter and Waew worked in 'unreached' villages in one of the provinces of Isaan, taking the gospel where there was no Christian witness. During that time, they saw ten village churches planted and took the gospel to a further three villages. In 2019, they returned to New Zealand to assist with the care of Peter's elderly mother. They have two adult sons and live and work in Hamilton.

Contents

Introduction	9
Setting the Stage: Is Thailand a Country Resistant to the Gospel?	11
Are Mass Evangelism or Church Planting Movements the Key for Thailand?	25
Understanding Buddhism is a Key	33
Key Ministry Principles for Reaching Isaan Folk Buddhists	45
Keys We Discovered for Starting a Seeker Meeting	73
The Gospel Produces Fruit	85
Keys in the Cultural Traditions that Can Open the Door to the Gospel	101
The Key of Prayer	113
The Call of God to Missions	125
Recommended Reading	133

Introduction

This book was not written to highlight what we have done in the past, but rather to assist those who are coming after, as they endeavour to follow the call of God to bring the gospel to the people of Northeast Thailand.

The Apostle Paul wrote: 'The god of this age has blinded the minds of unbelievers, so that they cannot see the light of the gospel of the glory of Christ...' (2 Corinthians 4:4). This statement equally describes the state of Buddhists in Thailand, who are blinded by a religious and cultural tradition that has left them not only in ignorance, but for many, deadened to the simple truths of the gospel.

There are keys in every culture for the pathway of the gospel message of Jesus Christ to pass with the least resistance. Finding those keys under the inspiration of the Holy Spirit is what missionaries need to do so that they have a path to connect to the thinking of the people they are trying to reach.

When Paul went to Athens (Acts 17), he was invited to speak at the Areopagus to an assembly of Stoic and Epicurean philosophers. Paul chooses his words very carefully. He did not preach the same sermon he had preached at the synagogue at Berea only a few days earlier. No, shaped under the inspiration of the Holy Spirit in a very carefully crafted message that followed philosophical conventions, he demonstrated his knowledge of their belief system. Furthermore, he used quotes from Greek poets to aid his message. While the result may not have been as successful as in other places, he proclaimed the gospel, and a few people believed and became followers. The key point is that Paul understood the culture and the religion of the people he was trying to reach. And certainly, when he preached in synagogues to Jews, he was doing the same. However, in Athens, it was 'cross-cultural evangelism' such as many missionaries will face in Thailand.

Those of us God has called to bring his Good News to Thailand also need to understand both the religion and the culture of Thailand. It is our hope this small book will help readers to gain a fuller understanding of both, whether they go, or stay home, pray and support.

Peter & Waew Martyn
May 2022

CHAPTER 1

Setting the Stage: Is Thailand a Country Resistant to the Gospel?

Any study of Christianity in the nation of Thailand is likely to cause nightmares for a church growth expert. If the evidence is in the statistics, the figures look bad.

This Buddhist nation of approximately 69 million people, which is relatively peaceful and kind to Christians, has been blessed with 500 years of Christian witness and yet has a Christian population barely over 1%.

Even the Muslim population is between 4-5%, so Christians are running a poor third place. Of that 1% (let's say 700,000), approximately half are Catholic and the other half Protestant.

The Joshua Project research initiative estimates that the evangelical church in Thailand numbers around 0.65% of the total population. This means only about 450,000 people attend a church that believes in actively proclaiming the gospel. However, there is some good news. The Joshua Project also put the evangelical annual growth rate at 3.6%, which does exceed the national population growth rate of 0.9% per annum. Still, it is snail's pace progress, and currently probably only 0.3% of the Thai population are ethnic Thai evangelical Christians.

More gloomy data can be found on the Operation World website, where they point out that of the 7,415 Tambon (or sub-districts of Thailand), more than 6,000 do not have even one church. And these Tambon host a total of 80,000 villages.

Then there is the bizarre statistic that 50% of these evangelical Thai Christians are not actually ethnic Thai at all, but tribal people also common to Burma, Laos, China and Vietnam, who have migrated from Southwest China in the last 200 years. These tribal groups only make up 5% of the total Thai population (some are not Thai citizens). So, 50% of Protestant Christians come out of only 5% of the population. This might not be so bad if they were evenly distributed over the country, but they are not. These evangelical Christians are all congregated in the three northern provinces of Chiang Mai, Chiang Rai and Mae Hong Son. In fact, the Mae Hong Son province is the only majority Christian province in Thailand, but the population is only about 50,000.

Perhaps unsurprisingly, Christian workers and missionaries have also now congregated in Northern Thailand. 70% of full-time Christian workers and missionaries are found in the three northern provinces, Chiang Mai having the highest density of full-time Christian workers in Thailand. You are more likely to bump into a Western missionary in Chiang Mai than in any other place in the country.

Meanwhile in the northeast region of Isaan, where 22 million people live, Christians make up only 0.1% of the population, with very few Christian workers and missionaries. This is one of the regions least touched by the gospel. There is a similar imbalance in Christian witness in the south of Thailand, in what is a mainly Muslim region.

Reaching the harder-to-get fruit

It is a disturbing fact that in the Isaan region, many villages and towns have no Christian witness at all. The rural areas are worst affected than the urban areas, and so the Isaan people are like the hard-to-reach fruit on a mango tree. Extra effort is required in method and determination. The fruit, however, is good and worth the effort.

In Thailand, the 'low-hanging fruit' has already been harvested. As mentioned, statistics tell us that 70% of Thai Christians are found living in the three adjoining northern provinces of Chiang Mai, Chiang Rai and Mae Hong Song.

Of these northern Christians, most are what are known as 'Hill Tribe' peoples. They have been open to the gospel, and generations of missionaries have worked with them as they were the most responsive to Christianity. These tribes were animist rather than Buddhist and as such, are a group that has always been less resistant to the gospel. They were the 'low-hanging fruit,' where early advances of Christianity were made. It has been observed in other countries that animist people groups are 'easier' to reach than people groups where there is a religion based on sacred texts and a highly organised priesthood and temple structure, such as Islam and Hinduism.

Buddhism is the third religion where the gospel has struggled to make inroads, with the exception being in Korea. The other 'easier' group harvested in Thailand in the early years were the Bangkok Chinese immigrants. They were also 'low hanging fruit.'

Today, the 'Tree of Thailand' still has much fruit to gather, but the low-hanging fruit is gone. What's left is the harder-to-reach fruit: ethnic groups like the Isaan, the southern Thai Muslims and the majority lowland Buddhists. Churches and mission organisations are only starting to wake up to this significant fact.

The good news about the Good News is that if presented correctly, diligently and repeatedly, the harder-to-reach fruit can be won for Christ. We've seen it happen. Failure that has discouraged local Christians and some missionaries is usually due to the approach used and sometimes the lack of effort.

A little Thai church history

It was Portuguese Catholic missionaries that first brought the Good News to the Kingdom of Thailand in the 16th Century. The early Catholic churches were established in Bangkok under royal permission but in reality, mainly served the Chinese immigrant population and European traders. These early missionaries saw very little progress in reaching ethnic Thai Buddhists.

In 1780, French missionaries were allowed to enter Thailand by King Taksin, and he helped them build a church. By the early 19th Century, there were estimated to be about 1,000 Christians in Bangkok, mainly Catholic descendants of Portuguese traders who had intermarried with Thai and ethnic Chinese.

Protestant missionaries didn't arrive in Thailand until 1828, and they ran into the same resistance to the gospel that the Catholics had experienced. There has been a continuous presence of American missionaries in Thailand since 1833, but after 18 years of work, this original team of 22 missionaries had failed to see one Thai convert. While their evangelism was largely unsuccessful, they greatly assisted in the modernisation of the country. American missionaries brought in the first printing press in 1835 and did important work getting the Bible printed in Thai.

King Mongkut (of *The King and I* fame) learnt English from the missionaries but is quoted as having said, 'What you teach them to do is admirable, but what you teach them to believe is foolish.' He saw no problem with allowing missionaries to operate in the country as he didn't seem to believe Buddhism was at risk of being displaced by Christianity.

The Thai church grew slowly in the early 20th Century. During World War Two, Thailand was occupied by the Japanese, who persecuted Thai Christians. They saw Christianity as a Western colonial religion and tried during the war years to cause believers to recant their faith and return to Buddhism. In this they caused quite some damage to Christianity, with significant numbers of Thai people dropping out of churches, including the moderator of the Thai Presbyterian Church. After the Japanese surrender, some of those who had recanted their faith returned, and in some churches, there was debate about whether they should be welcomed back.

Greater success came later in the northern provinces, particularly where Protestant missionaries focused on bringing the gospel to animist Hill Tribe peoples, who were much more receptive than the ethnic Thai Buddhists. Today there are significant numbers of Christians among tribes such as the Karen, Lisu, Hmong and Akha. The situation in the neighbouring country of Laos is very similar, with Christianity found mainly among Hill Tribe groups but few believers among the lowland Buddhist ethnic Lao people.

The ethnic lowland Thai have been much harder to reach with the gospel, partly because of the hold that Buddhist tradition has over Thai people, but also because of the prevalent perception that to become a Christian means to abandon Thai ways. Christianity has long struggled to shake off the popular idea that it is a 'foreign' religion, which is a little ironic given the origins of Buddhism.

There is a popular saying amongst Thai that is 'to be Thai is to be Buddhist.' That sentiment is no doubt encouraged by Buddhist monks who have watched missionaries warily for 500 years. Even though to be born Thai means to be born Buddhist, the average Thai person is as much a nominal Buddhist as many in the West are nominal Christians who rarely darken the doorway of a church.

Thai people follow many of the rituals of Buddhism but mostly only attempt to obey the Five Precepts of Buddhism, basically the absolute minimum needed to be called a Buddhist. These precepts are: (1) Refrain from killing living things, (2) Refrain from stealing, (3) Refrain from sexual misconduct (adultery), (4) Refrain from wrong speech (lies, slander), and (5) Refrain from alcohol and intoxicants.

Talk with many Thai Buddhists and they will openly agree that they cannot follow all the Five Precepts, in much the same way a nominal Christian might admit they cannot keep all the Ten Commandments.

It seems odd that a country with a majority religion so laid back that apostates are rarely under threat of violence should have such a hold over its adherents. Certainly, fear of death or disownment by family is not a common feature, but there still is constant pressure on Christian converts to return to Buddhism by family, friends and, of course, monks.

This slow progress of evangelisation may be the reason why the Catholic Church in Thailand no longer aims to convert the Buddhist population. They are quite open about this and seem to be content to exist on biological growth from their existing church members. These days, Catholic outreaches in Thailand are solely mercy ministry, not evangelism.

To be fair, there are some parallels here with the work of the Protestant mission organisations in India in the 19th Century. Progress for the gospel there was only found amongst the very lowest caste, and eventually, the mission agencies changed tack and founded hospital outreaches and schools.

Something similar happened in Thailand. Both Catholic and Protestant churches and mission agencies have established hospitals and schools in the last 100 years. There are approximately 350 'Christian' schools in Thailand, and most would be Catholic schools. These are private schools for fee-paying students, and the most prestigious ones are certain Catholic schools in Bangkok. Their students come not from poor slum-dwelling families but from the wealthy Thai Buddhist elite. Members of the royal family and politicians have also been educated at Catholic schools. It would seem most of the students are from Buddhist households. Waew's brother is a staunch Buddhist but is quite happy to have his children attend a Catholic school.

So, despite having nuns for teachers and religious statues depicting Jesus and Mary in the school grounds, it seems very few students from Buddhist families become followers of Jesus Christ, but then that doesn't seem to have been the plan in the establishment of these schools.

Prayer movement organisation, Operation World, states the encouraging news on their website that 'national church leaders have a bold goal to reach every one of Thailand's 80,000 villages and neighbourhoods with the gospel.'

It is good to have goals. It is even better to have a strategy to reach that goal. Unfortunately, we have heard this sort of thing before. We recall during our time in Thailand that every few years, a national inter-denominational conference of Protestant churches would end with a bold growth vision statement.

Back in 2016, the growth plan for the Thai National churches was a goal for there to be 'two million Thai Christians by 2020.' That was an ambitious goal, a faith-stretching goal. At the time, the population was 65 million, and there were only about 500,000 Christians in the country. 400% growth in four years was required to achieve the target. We now know this didn't happen.

In fact, during our 13 years working in rural villages, we rarely saw any workers from local churches out doing evangelism or heard about any visits from people from a church.

Occasionally a group from a church in the city would pass through a village, handing out tracts, usually around Christmas time, but they rarely returned.

Observations about the Thai church today

It must be awkward being a national leader of one of the Thai church denominations. If they attended an Asian regional conference with other Asian Christian leaders, they might hear how South Korea, another Buddhist country, is now 20% Christian. Even Muslim Indonesia has a higher percentage of Christians than Thailand. The question might be thought, but certainly not spoken, 'What have you guys been doing?' This is possibly why the Evangelical Fellowship churches in Thailand regularly have bold growth goals, as it suggests something is being done.

The reason for the inactivity, we believe, is a mixture of cultural reticence to avoid conflict, and laziness. In Thai culture, people try to avoid awkward situations where disagreement or conflict could result. This presents a problem when they are Christians, and a pastor or missionary tells them they should be involved in evangelism. To many Thai Christians, the prospect of even suggesting to someone they should think about another religion is a stumbling block. When Waew was a student at a discipleship course in Thailand, they had times of outreach when they went out onto the streets to 'witness.' This didn't faze Waew at all, in part due to her fearless, outgoing personality. On these outreaches, the leaders were the most timid and pushed her to the front when it came to speaking to a stranger. This is fairly typical in our observation of Thai Christians in the cities.

There could also be an element of 'let the missionaries do it' in the thinking of the Thai church. Foreign missionaries have been in the country for so long, pioneering all the evangelism works that the church is quite happy to leave them to it.

It cannot be simply a case of lack of training as Thailand has many very good Bible colleges training future pastors. There are many scholarly pastors and church leaders in the Thai church.

What they do seem to lack is evangelists. One large ministry in Thailand with over 300 staff runs various training courses in discipleship, biblical studies, and family ministries, but no focused school of evangelism.

There is an example of a Thai church that broke the mold. For a time, The Hope of Bangkok Church, later called the Hope Church, was an example of Thai Christians stepping outside comfort zones and getting serious about witnessing their faith. The church grew rapidly and was the fastest growing denomination for a time until moral failure at the leadership level caused it to split and divide. It has been reported that the founder of the church movement (who was often quoted in church growth books published during the 1990s) now doesn't even describe himself as a Christian.

It is interesting that the Hope Church was an indigenous church, not begun by missionaries, but would generally fit into the 'international charismatic' category with Western worship songs, such as Hillsong, translated into Thai. A little too controlling for our liking and a little too 'Western' in style, although the doctrine was sound, based on what we heard when we visited occasionally. But laziness in personal witnessing was not something they could be accused of; if anything, they were perhaps rather too pushy. But at least the Hope people were committed.

Another problem in the Protestant church is nominalism. In countries where your identity is linked to your religion and your national ID card lists your religion, children from Christian households are told from a young age that they are 'Christian.' When they go to school, they are told to 'tell the other kids and the teacher you are Christian.' The reason they are told this is so they might be excused from Buddhist ceremonies held at school. But this thinking can undermine the gospel. As we know, we are not Christians by virtue of being born into a Christian family.

Paul wrote, 'And if anyone does not have the Spirit of Christ, they do not belong to Christ' (Roman 8:9). We are Christian because of the decisions we have made personally and the faith we have in Jesus Christ. This misunderstanding is widespread in the Thai church and, for that matter, the church in Indonesia, Malaysia and other Asian countries where it is a minority faith.

The average Thai church congregation size in urban areas is only about 30 members. Churches often rely on biological growth rather than growth through evangelism and new converts to keep ticking over, and the true gospel, 'You must be born again,' is not preached. In many churches, the members may all be from Christian families, with few or none who are former Buddhists who have been saved.

This is a problem in so far as it means the Christians don't fully understand Buddhism, and so they don't have a testimony to tell why they left Buddhism and now follow Jesus. Without a conversion testimony, and limited knowledge of the Buddhist life, those points of understanding and rapport are missing, and it is much harder for them to present the gospel in a way that will be received.

We gained the impression when meeting local (primarily urban) Christians and pastors that they were quite happy for missionaries to keep coming to Thailand to do evangelism. We suspected the reason was that it meant they could avoid doing it themselves.

As far as church leadership is concerned, there is an unfortunate tendency toward dynastic pastorships, where the role of pastor is passed from father to son, rather like the Old Testament priesthood. The problem here is that sometimes the son can resemble a 'son of Eli' and not be worthy of the ministry. The problem often arises when the pastor is nearing retirement age and the family has no home other than the church building. This seems to be quite common with Thai city churches. The solution is to send one son to Bible College, and they can then succeed their father as pastor. The elderly parents can then remain living on the church premises.

We have personal knowledge of this type of situation in a city Pentecostal church we once attended. The father was the pastor, and the family lived on the church premises. Unfortunately, in the case we are familiar with, it soon became clear the son was a womaniser who led a double life. The church was scandalised, and his marriage to a nice Christian girl from the church broke up.

A missionary friend in a discipling ministry for new believers told us the story of a young man they sponsored through a Bangkok Bible College. He was a country boy from a Buddhist family background, but at Bible College, his fellow students were all the sons of pastors. He was shocked to discover at night the pastors' sons were climbing out of the college hostel window to visit Hostess Go Go bars. That is where the Thai churches' future leaders were coming from. The country boy said he doubted if they were saved.

When Thai people do attempt evangelism, there is often a problem with the message. Many Thai city churches are very poor at explaining the gospel. When there are visitors or someone has brought along a non-Christian friend or family member to a church meeting, there is often excessive zeal to get them up to the front of the church to pray a two-minute sinner's prayer. And this is without even explaining repentance or what it means to be a follower of Jesus. We have seen this many times visiting a city church. The new person prodded to the front understands little of what is going on and usually doesn't return the following Sunday. They just become another Thai inoculated against the gospel.

Another common situation observed is the seeker has a wrong God concept. They see the Christian God like one of the deities associated with Buddhism, where you worship and make an offering to get a prayer answered. To know God and to have a relationship with the Creator is not explained or understood. People come to a church wanting a prayer answered, and if it's not, they will fall away. They may have an understanding of being a sinner, but Buddhism has taught them that it can be dealt with through good works. Failure to see a prayer answered is a leading cause of loss of faith. We have seen this ourselves with our village church work.

In Thai culture, there is a custom of 'patronage,' that is, the ordinary folks will align themselves with a figure of power. In historical times, it would have been a local chief or prince. It is similar to the European feudal concept, where allegiance to that leader means they will also protect and provide for you. This continues in Thai politics, where politicians cultivate a power base of support from villages or towns and they regularly visit (near election time) to hand out wads of bank notes, in exchange for the people's votes!

Something similar is present in the Thai church and among the attitude of new Christians, particularly those from a Buddhist background. Customary respect for leadership authority figures and the need for a patron causes foreign missionaries to be very quickly lined up by local Christians as a potential patron, a source of employment and financial support, and even future retirement security. One situation for a ministry to be careful of is using a local Christian as a 'name' on a land title. Years down the track, problems can arise over expectations.

For this dependency reason, we decided early on we wouldn't, as a rule, pay or employ anyone for a leadership role in village churches. Our goal was for the people to look to God and their local church community, rather than to the missionary or an overseas church for their needs, and work as a 'tentmaker' if necessary. This strategy works well in a rural context anyway, as leaders are often farmers.

Difficult as it is to air issues like what we have covered in this section, we felt it was important that new workers heading to ministry in Thailand had some idea of what to expect when they arrive in Thailand. Some of the things we have discussed are not at all widely talked about and we were never told about what to expect with regards the National Church before we began ministry work in Thailand. Knowing what to expect from the local church will enable new workers to act wisely in all their interactions.

CHAPTER 2

Are Mass Evangelism or Church Planting Movements the Key for Thailand?

Thailand has had missionaries for a long time, and various approaches to presenting the gospel have been tried. From the 1960s, the mass evangelism crusade event strategy has been used. In the early days, large crowds could be pulled into one of these rallies, but this approach has increasingly become less effective.

We went along to observe several mass evangelism events during our ministry years in Thailand. The evangelist was always from an overseas ministry, relying on a local partner church or churches to provide support and backup while the ministry funds the event. Generally, Thai churches are happy to do this. Waew offered her services as a translator to one mission from a Scandinavian country, so we have an inside perspective of how the crusade events work.

In this example from the early 2000s, the evangelist arrived in Northeast Thailand fresh from a crusade in Africa, where it was reported that 30,000 people attended and many were healed. Before he arrived, an advance team came to liaise with local churches and gain their assistance. Several churches provided people who could act as translators. A huge stage was constructed in a public park in the city (funded by the ministry) and for weeks before the crusade, banners hung across the roads in the city announcing, 'Signs and Wonders Festival.' Churches that were in support distributed untold flier advertisements also headed 'Signs and Wonders Festival.'

Three evening meetings were scheduled, and the first was prefixed by a parade down the main street with a band leading and at the rear the evangelist riding an elephant, causing much interest to be generated.

On the first day of the outreach, a moderate-sized crowd gathered. I tried to estimate numbers and my count came to about 2,000 people. We met many Christians at the event, and some had come from cities 100 to 200 kilometres away. On one night, we brought about 20 people from two villages where we had planted churches that year in a truck we had hired.

During the meeting, the evangelist preached a gospel message and, rather simply, told the crowd if they were sick or needed healing, to lay hands on themselves and he would pray for everyone. This he did, then he asked if people had been healed to come forward and testify to that healing. A large stream of people came forward and spoke to the crowd. The translator was busy explaining to the evangelist what was happening. Many gave testimonies of instant healings.

Next, the evangelist invited those wishing to receive salvation to come forward. About a quarter of the crowd moved forward, including the people we had brought from the village and some others we recognised as local Christians. I asked Waew, 'Why are they going forward? They are already saved!' Her answer was that they just wanted to be blessed by the man of God. This was an interesting observation of what we had noticed before in city churches when an overseas pastor was ministering.

Over the following two nights, slightly smaller crowds attended; around 1,500 people, with less response. The overseas team was apparently surprised not more came, the level of interest being much lower than they had experienced in Africa. But this was their first experience of evangelism in a Buddhist country.

Waew said when she was working with some American counsellors, she would translate what they said and what the salvation responder said. One time, Waew, giving the benefit of her own knowledge of God's salvation plan, spoke directly to the Thai person who had come forward. She was immediately rebuked by the counsellors who said, 'You don't talk to people. You only translate!'

After the outreach, a team was left in the city and they quickly announced the formation of an international church on the campus of a city university, with meetings in English and Thai. Several local translators joined the team in this new city church, leaving existing church positions as assistant pastors and workers in local ministries. This caused much grief and hurt in local city churches, as the overseas ministry had promised local churches that they wouldn't plant a church after the outreach but would funnel all growth into existing local churches.

In the years that followed, we never met anyone who said they had become a Christian at the outreach in the park in 2006. As for the follow-up the local churches were supposed to do, local pastors we spoke to said they tried to follow up, but contact information collected on the night was often incomplete or incorrect, or when they visited, no one was home. The net effect seemed to be some demonstration of God's grace by healing, but growth for the Kingdom of God was less tangible.

In a way, it didn't really surprise us. We had also come across Thai Buddhists who would gratefully receive a healing from the 'Christian God' but saw no need to change their allegiance to God and away from the Buddha. Thai people are often willing to add another deity to their worship, and so syncretism is always a potential outcome from some Buddhist hearers of the gospel.

A few years later we went to another mass evangelism event

held in a city in a neighbouring province. It was also organised by an international ministry with a foreign evangelist and held at a sports ground. What we saw was similar to the previous events. People responded to the message, but we had a real concern local churches, which were small, would not be able to follow up or disciple the people who responded.

As another missionary once said to us, the day of mass evangelism events is over for Thailand. They have not been an effective way to present the gospel and grow the local church.

Are church planting movements the key?

Church Planting Movements (CPMs) is a term coined by David Garrison in his 1999 published book, *Church Planting Movements: How God is Redeeming a Lost World*. In the book, Garrison describes a CPM as 'rapidly multiplying indigenous churches planting churches that sweep across a people group or population segment.' The book described incredibly fast-growing and multiplying churches all powered by the Holy Spirit. There were stories of new believers planting churches after being only a few months in the Lord and of thousands being reached with the gospel within a year.

In the early 2000s, when Waew and I were contemplating a 'call of God' to return to Thailand as missionaries, we became very interested in this new phenomenon. Back then, there was a buzz in missions circles, and you couldn't talk about missions and not mention CPMs. For many missiologists, the CPM was the breakthrough, a silver bullet to seeing the world finally reached for Christ.

We shared the enthusiasm and hoped to see a CPM released in rural Thailand in the villages we were targeting when we arrived in 2006. We had already done some research and discovered there had been a conference focusing on CPMs in Thailand a few years earlier.

When we arrived and spoke with foreign missionaries in the Northeast, there was great excitement amongst workers, and it seemed everyone wanted to see a CPM released. One American missionary couple who had already worked in Thailand for 20 years told us their role now was to mentor Thai church pastors to release CPMs in the region. But they themselves had so far never seen a CPM in Thailand. We also discovered that the American Southern Baptist Church Mission Board (who send the largest number of long-term missionaries to Thailand) had adopted CPMs exclusively as their global mission's strategy. In other words, the ministry focus of all Southern Baptist missionaries was now seeing CPMs released. Now this meant that they had to train local believers, as a CPM is very much about letting the local workers do the work. It had to be indigenous-led, with foreign workers in a coaching role.

We began ministry within six months of arriving in Thailand, visiting unreached villages. The goal was to plant a church, but also to encourage and work towards seeing a CPM eventually begin through these new believers. We saw early results of God moving in lives, and within a year had planted the first church of eight to ten people in a village. A CPM requires trained and motivated workers going out and taking the gospel to other people in other villages. This worked in India, but would it work in Thailand?

It seemed everyone in the foreign missions' community was talking about and promoting CPMs, but no one had seen one. One of the challenges in seeing such a multiplying movement from new believers in house churches was that not many new believers were willing to take on the training and task of taking the gospel to others. It might be easier with more mature believers such as would be found in city churches, but even there we didn't hear of anything like a CPM event occurring.

With any house church, where the number of people is small (typically the average size of the house churches we worked with was a dozen people), the number of potential leaders (those willing to lead) may also be small. And they may not be willing or ready to take on a leadership role for several years after salvation. What we were finding was the ideal held up by the CMP theory was not easily achieved. One CPM document we saw had a list of over 20 factors that when present would lead to a release of a CPM. The more we read, the more it began to sound like a formula. If you have A, B, C etc, it will result in a CMP occurring. If it doesn't occur, you haven't followed the plan.

By now, our perception of the reported phenomenon of CPMs was simply as a move of the Holy Spirit in what He wanted to do in a particular people group at a particular time. Training people to release CPMs seemed a little like holding a miracle-working seminar. If it was not God's will at that time, it wasn't going to happen. It's good to train people to be witnesses of their faith, but expectation from trainers of breathless reports of 'hundreds saved' could lead to unwanted outcomes, particularly with workers financially supported by that same missionary and being physically separated from their mentor, i.e. with little oversight.

After a couple of years of not hearing about any CPMs occurring locally, we began an internet search to see if we could pick up any news. We found reports of a Thai couple that were apparently in the middle of a CPM. From a Bangkok church, they received some training at a conference on CPMs in Thailand. They were being mentored by a Western missionary who gave regular updates on their ministry website. At one point it was said that 50,000 converts had come out of this CPM already. A typical report would mention 4,000 baptisms in the last year. If this was true, it was incredible church growth previously unseen in Thai church history. I contacted the missionary to seek further information. They themselves were relying on reports conveyed to them, but at 50,000 CPM converts, the church numbers exceeded the entire Thai Assembly of God Church at the time.

We made enquiries locally. Had anyone heard of this new CPM? Nobody had, and certainly in our province, we saw no evidence of it. Sometime later, I made contact with an American missionary who was a CPM trainer working with a small church in a corner of the Northeast region. I asked him about this CPM. He had actually visited the Thai couple leading it and spent a few days with them. He said he was concerned about a few things he saw and gave them some recommendations for changes in the way they did things.

In a nutshell, he described what he saw as 'pseudo-Christian,' which confirmed what we had suspected. Another missionary contact told us he had also visited this CPM couple where he heard that the church planters were trained and sent out to visit villages. Once they had found a 'person of peace' who received the gospel, they were discipled over a few weeks and commissioned to go out themselves to another village, with the promise from the trainer to 'see you in six months.' That lack of ongoing discipling of the CPM worker concerned us.

Around 2019, this same missionary, who we knew well and who had a rural village church planting focus, began training some of their people in CPM techniques. They also had another missionary CPM expert mentoring them in the training. While some of these trained people have gone out, presumably with greater confidence in the message, we haven't yet heard any news of a CPM breaking out.

In the 13 years we were in Thailand, we saw new missionaries arriving and aiming to see a CPM released. It didn't happen, and mostly after three or four years they returned home, presumably much disappointed.

CPMs may happen one day when the Holy Spirit decides the time is right, but to have CPMs as the only 'tool in the box' strategy seems unwise. As Paul wrote, 'I have become all things to all men so that by *all means* I might save some' (1 Corinthians 9:22). CPMs might be one of those means, but then again, other ministry approaches might also be the way (or key) God chooses to move in the near future in Thailand. Openness to all opportunities to communicate the gospel in ways the cultural group can be best reached is the key point.

CHAPTER 3

Understanding Buddhism is a Key

This chapter gives a brief overview and introduction of Buddhism in order to aid an understanding of the Buddhist worldview prevalent in Thailand.

Siddharta Gautama (563-483 BC) was the founder of Buddhism. What is described of his life from the Tripitaka scriptures (written hundreds of years after his life) is that he was from a wealthy, noble family in North India and lived a sheltered life in his early years. One day when out and about, he became aware of the problem of suffering. He decided there and then to leave behind his wife and child and a life of comfort to go and search for an answer.

At first, he decided to study with the Hindu Brahmin hermits, but they could not show him how to escape the cycle of reincarnations. He then tried living as an ascetic hermit himself for several years but was disappointed to realise this had not helped him reach his goal.

It was after a long period of meditation that Gautama was convinced he had reached enlightenment. Thereafter, he was given the title 'Buddha,' meaning 'the enlightened one.'

Over the following centuries, two distinct schools of Buddhism emerged, Theravada and Mahayana. It is Theravada Buddhism that claims to be more authentic to Gautama's teaching, while Mahayana developed later and began to regard the Buddha as an eternal god-like being. They also developed a doctrine of bodhisattvas, who are semi-divine beings on the way to enlightenment who look out for the needs of ordinary Buddhists. Mahayana is now the main school of Buddhism in terms of popularity, and adherents are mainly centred in China and Tibet.

In Thailand and Sri Lanka, however, most Buddhists are adherents of Theravada Buddhism. There is a historical link between these two outposts of Theravada Buddhism, with the teachings likely introduced into Thailand by travelling Buddhist monks from Sri Lanka.

Important doctrines in Thai Buddhism

After his enlightenment, Gautama began to proclaim his 'four noble truths':

1) Suffering. Life is basically a journey of suffering.
2) Desire is the cause of suffering. This would include the desire for possessions, pleasure and enjoyment.
3) Suffering ends when desire ends. When desire for things, lust and passion for life ends, then suffering will also end.
4) The path to ending suffering is the 'Eightfold Path.'

The Eightfold Path

Buddhists will seek to end suffering by following these eight stepping stones:

1) Right Views
2) Right Aspirations

3) Right Speech
4) Right Conduct
5) Right Occupation
6) Right Effort
7) Right Awareness
8) Right Concentration

This last step involves concentrating on one object, clearing the mind of distractions, then going beyond pleasure and pain into a transcending state of consciousness, finally reaching a point of enlightenment, as the Buddha did.

Karma and reincarnation

All Buddhists believe in reincarnation, the idea that death leads to rebirth into another life on earth, possibly in different circumstances. Whether the next life is better and more comfortable is based on what you did in the last life. Buddhists will frequently have on their mind that if they are not careful and don't follow the eight precepts, their next life could be worse than what they live now, which provides food for thought and motivation.

The idea of reaching Nirvana is dismissed as unrealistic by most lay Buddhists. This sort of enlightenment is only attainable, they believe, for full-time monks and those who are exceptionally diligent. A much more 'livable Buddhism' offers the path of building up good karma during your life to offset the bad deeds, sins and failures to follow the Buddha's teaching closely. This is also called 'merit-making' and is by far the most common form of Buddhist practice followed by Thai people. Loosely, merit-making is 'doing good,' but it carries more power when directed to the organisation of the Buddhist religion.

The first way an average Thai person gains merit is by looking after the monks. This involves giving food to monks as they walk the streets early in the mornings. The monks make the rounds daily to give the local population the opportunity to give directly to them, and so gain merit or good karma. They can also gain merit by taking part in temple ceremonies and giving donations to building works at the temple. *It is these rituals to make merit that are the most important religious practice of Thai people.* It is essentially a works-based religion.

Temple ceremonies

In villages, the temple is the hub of the village. Every village in Thailand, all 80,000 of them, has a Buddhist temple, so there is both the opportunity and the expectation that all inhabitants will take part in temple ceremonies. It is important to consider this with regards to the situation for any Christians that might be in that village or any converts.

The situation is often different in cities, however. Many people now don't go to the temple regularly or at all, and this can remain unnoticed in the cities. This is something that is harder to do in a village where everyone knows everyone else, and so it could be said that Buddhism is stronger in rural areas, certainly it is more traditional.

There are five major Buddhist festivals per year. The first is Visakha Pula, which commemorates the birth, enlightenment and death of the Buddha. The second is Magha Puja, a commemoration of the day when 1,250 disciples of Buddha gathered three months before he died. The third is Khaw Pansa, the beginning of the Buddhist lent. It coincides with the beginning of the wet season and the start of preparing the land for rice growing. During this three-month period, monks are not allowed to sleep outside the temple compound and in many villages don't go out to collect alms. The villagers bring food to the temple during these months.

This period is an auspicious time for men to enter the monkhood, and most induction ceremonies will occur around Khaw Pansa. Joining the monkhood is a merit-making occasion, and a man may become a monk for as little as three months prior to starting a secular job or career. Becoming a monk is also a way that a man can make merit for his mother, which is significant as in Buddhism, women cannot attain the same heights as men. This period ends with the festival of Ohk Pansa, or the end of Pansa.

The fifth main festival is Phra Kathin, during which the laity will make donations of robes for monks to wear, another good karma opportunity.

House ceremonies

There are three occasions when monks may be invited to a residential home: weddings, funerals, and the blessing of a new house.

The Buddha never provided any guidance on funeral proceedings, but as earlier religious practice (pre-Buddhism) certainly would have had a ceremony, the monks in Thailand have developed one.

Funerals can last a week, and the body of the deceased is transferred to an ice-packed box fairly quickly in view of the climate. Cremation at the temple would occur some days later.

At these house ceremonies, several seated monks would chant Buddhist scriptures, gifts would be given to them, holy water sprinkled, and incense sticks burnt.

Folk Buddhism is the main practice in Northeast Thailand

The term 'Folk Buddhism' refers to the practice of merging orthodox Buddhist ideas with animist traditions and beliefs. As well as the ritual ceremonies and making of merit, the Buddhism of Northeast Thailand is closely associated with animism, the worship of various unseen spirits (Phi) and their appeasement. Much of what takes place in the name of Buddhism in the northeast region is not pure Buddhism, but a carrying on of an earlier spirit-worshipping religion of ancestors. And in a sense, for most common people, the spirit aspect is more important and a more frequent focus in their life than the 'eightfold path.' Engaging with the spirit world is all about ensuring present needs are met rather than some distant afterlife need.

The Buddha didn't deny the idea of gods and spirits, but taught they were not relevant to gaining enlightenment. This merging of religious practices forms what is described as Folk Buddhism. There are also aspects of Brahmanism, seeking help from angel beings or gods for prosperity, good health and good luck. Usually, it is associated with cycles of life and the agricultural calendar. These ideas may originate with the earlier Khmer rulers from the Middle Ages.

Animism, in contrast, deals with minor, localised spirits that must be appeased to bring success in life. There are shaman figures called Maw Phi (literally 'spirit doctors') in the Isaan language, who manipulate the spirits to bring healing to the sick. Some strange practices take place to achieve the results sought by a customer by the Maw Phi, including the use of alcohol, dancing, smoking, trances and magic. Some of the practitioners are themselves Buddhist monks, but no one finds this odd.

Black magic is closely associated, and it is not uncommon for Maw Phi to be contracted to put curses on people. Other people use spells to make them attractive to others. Some men will seek magic to make women attracted to them. Fraudsters might use magic to deceive others.

Once we visited a Dutch missionary family who had been in Thailand for quite a few years. As we were leaving, our attention was drawn to the severed black wing of a rooster lying on the driveway outside their house.

'Someone has left one of those three times, is it magic?' they asked Waew. She confirmed it was. Later, as we drove away, she told me the fuller answer. Someone was trying to drive them out of the village using magic. It seemed odd that the Dutch missionaries didn't know that.

Lucky amulets

The use of amulets is the commonly seen visual sign of Folk Buddhism. Walk along any street in Thailand and you won't go far before seeing a table set up for the sale of Buddha amulets. These small brass, copper or ceramic images of the Buddha on a chain to be worn around the neck are very popular. It is believed the good ones (and fakes exist!) convey power and protection to the wearer. Most Buddhist Thai men will wear one of these amulets, sometimes several on a chain. They believe the amount of power of the amulet depends on various factors, including the type of magic spell used by the maker (often monks) and which auspicious monk blessed the amulet. Buyers examine the wares, often with a jeweller's magnifying glass, to authenticate an original, powerful amulet. Many temples supplement their income by making amulets for the masses.

When we arrived in Thailand in 2006, it coincided with an amulet craze that began at a temple in the south of Thailand. These large, round Jatukam amulets displaying the images of two legendary princes became a craze that lasted a year. People who bought them made claims of miraculous protection or miraculous wealth. Full-page advertisements in newspapers detailed the various types on offer from the increasingly wealthy temple.

Fortune-telling and spirit houses

Equally visible on the street corners of Northeast Thailand and much of the country are the fortune-tellers. Sometimes sitting at a table, other times on a mat on the ground, they wait for customers. Some are palm readers, others use other methods of divination.

Monks are often also fortune-tellers and will give advice on an auspicious date to begin a project such as a new house being built. They can also be involved in blessing the foundation pole of the house and gaining permission from the spirits of the land for the building of the house, and for the protection of the residents.

Spirit houses are also commonly seen in the yard beside a dwelling in Thailand. Often looking like a doll's house on a pole, the Spirit House might have tiny figures to keep the spirit company. The hope is the spirit will be content to live in the spirit house and won't bother the people in the house beside it. Offerings will be left in the spirit house, including a bottle of Coke or glass of Fanta, along with incense sticks and flowers.

Spirit houses are also commonly found in shops or outside large commercial premises like car dealerships and supermarkets, where they can take on the scale of mini mansions, often looking like a classical Thai temple.

The belief with these spirits is that their power is localised to the plot of land, village or even tree. Removal of a tree from a building site would involve complicated rituals to placate the spirit and offer alternative accommodation in the spirit house. It is believed that failure to provide a spirit house would bring bad luck onto the site and cause problems such as accidents later. Some workers may refuse to work on site without a spirit house.

In the Isaan villages where we worked, we noticed larger shrines to village spirits, often in the middle of the village or at the perimeter edge. These were for the 'ruling spirit of the village.' The shrines usually include a carved phallic post, similar to the Hindu Lingu idols seen in 14th Century Khmer laterite temples found throughout the region. We would often see an offering of a small amount of sticky rice wrapped in banana leaves or some joss sticks beside these shrines. Sometimes, balls of sticky rice were left on the concrete block wall of a perimeter fence outside a house.

Karma, face and status symbols

Visiting Asia for the first time in the 1980s was a shock for me (Peter), not because of the poverty but due to the extravagant display of the wealth of the rich. Growing up in New Zealand in the 1960s and '70s, I came from a country that was called an egalitarian society, where most people were at a similar level economically, and the few wealthy types tended to be discrete and not overly flashy in displaying it. The reverse was true in Asia. Those with wealth wanted others to know about it. This is tied up with the influence of the Buddhist idea of karma.

To the Buddhist who believes that good will come to the person who follows the Eightfold Path, wealth is the obvious outworking of good karma. Woven into this idea is the personal pride that is associated with 'face.' People will go to great effort to avoid 'losing face' or being embarrassed or humiliated. A sensitive person will try to avoid putting another person in a situation where they could lose face. When taking losing face into account, it can be seen why robust debate may be avoided and evangelism situations can become awkward.

To the Buddhist, the projected image of wealth and success is manifested in the trinkets of luxury. If they can, they will drive a Mercedes Benz car, which is seen across Asia as the most prestigious brand (some Thai even have the nickname Benz), wear a Rolex watch, and own other designer goods. These objects help to project their good karma. (The popularity of playing golf in Asian countries is often linked more to projected image of wealth than a love of sport.) The message is that they are wealthy because they have good karma accumulated from previous lives, and that is a powerful signal many, perhaps most, Buddhists will want to project. It also explains the often blasé attitude to poverty in Buddhist countries. Poor, lepers, and other disadvantaged people can be explained as being in that state due to bad karma in former lives. If it is their own fault, you can excuse yourself from not helping. And many do.

Sometimes people fake their wealth image. They may have the flash car and the flash watch but own few other assets and have a mountain of debt. That doesn't matter. The main point is other people think they have good karma and will respect them because of it. This also can explain why the Christian can be looked down upon if they are of modest means because, to the Buddhist mind, this reflects bad karma. Conversely, unearned respect is often immediately extended to 'Westerners,' who Thai people universally believe are rich, whether they are or not.

The Cult of Kings

The Kings of Thailand have long been regarded as semi-divine, and certainly by the time they die they will be venerated, if not fully worshipped. One favourite past king of note was King Chulalongkorn, who lived over a century ago and is credited for modernising the country and abolishing slavery. Most Thai houses will have a picture of the King on the wall to show respect for the monarchy, but often these images are associated with worship and gifts, and fruit and joss sticks will be in front of the portrait.

Conclusion

Our observation of Folk Buddhism in Isaan villages was that there was a whole lot more Folk than Buddhism when it came to what was most real in the lives of the rural people. The power that spirits have over people, or the fear of those spirits, was significant and more in mind than many of the Buddhist doctrines. People might be too scared to walk past a certain tree near their land at night because of spirits. One woman told us she once heard footsteps behind her at night while walking to her remote fields but turned and saw no one there.

Ephesians chapter 6 became a key scripture for us during our village work. Daily we put on the spiritual armour and went out mindful that we were invading the territory of invisible spirit powers that would seek to stop the Lord's work. We taught from this chapter regularly, as it was liberating for those in the village churches to discover that their heavenly father had provided the means to stand firm and resist the Devil and his schemes.

CHAPTER 4

Key Ministry Principles for Reaching Isaan Folk Buddhists

'As soon as the grain is ripe, he puts a sickle to it, because the harvest has come.' (Mark 4:29)

It's harvest time! The fields are ripe for harvest!

The rice harvest season, beginning in November every year, stirred our hearts to the core. We've spent months watching the rice paddy, or 'naa' as they are called in Thailand, change from young green plants to golden fields, with each plant bearing a yield.

Such a scene also inspired the Lord, as he used it as a frequent spiritual metaphor.

Everyone likes harvest time! As Christians we talk about 'harvest.' We wish more souls would be harvested for the Kingdom of God. We pray for harvest.

But here's the thing. To the farmer, harvest is the *culmination of his diligent work*. 'A farmer went out to sow his seed' (Matthew 13:3). He has broken the soil, turned the sods, harrowed the ground, sowed good seed; and then tended the seedlings by adding fertiliser, weeding, and protecting them from insect attack. After three to four months, he reaps the *fruits of his labour.* Farmers have an expectation of harvest, or they wouldn't sow! Harvest is the culmination of earlier labour.

It is the same in the spiritual realm. We can't expect to see harvest if we don't put in the time 'preparing the soil,' 'sowing good seed,' and supporting the growth of faith until we see the harvest yield of spiritual rebirth with those we have laboured for.

This is a timeless agricultural principle that is mirrored in the spiritual world. Let us view ourselves as 'farmers of the gospel,' and not just occasional, casual harvesters, but workers committed to being involved in all stages of seeing the lost coming to a saving knowledge of Jesus Christ.

But that will require the commitment of our time. 'A farmer went out...'

Partnership with God in the harvest

Bible-centred evangelism should be work done in close partnership with God. The Great Commission (Matthew 28:18-20) is constructed with three layers, rather like a sandwich. A top layer represents Jesus and his work: 'All authority in heaven and earth has been given to me;' a middle layer being us Christians and our appointed work: 'Therefore go and make disciples of the nations...;' and a bottom layer again representing Jesus: 'And surely I will be with you always to the very end of the age.'

Evangelism, therefore, is a partnership with God, where God is above and below and all around us – *Jesus' work/our work/Jesus' work*. And the partnership works like this: *He does His bit if we do our bit*. It really is quite simple.

He rebuilds people's lives. He saves and heals *as we teach what Jesus told us to teach*. If we obey what Jesus has already told us to do, He will come through and bring salvation, healing and blessings.

And what did Jesus tell us to teach? The same thing He proclaimed: the Cross and Good News of the Kingdom of God. And it's a partnership, *we proclaim, and He does the rest*.

So, in ministry, our work is to proclaim the Cross and the

Kingdom of God, and the Lord turns up and does the saving, the healing, the restoring, the blessing and the freeing from Satan's power.

Martin Luther described the partnership we have with God in this way. He said, 'All I have to do is proclaim the Good News of the Kingdom and sit back and watch God go to work.' That is a perfect picture of the God-intended partnership we have in advancing the Kingdom of God in the world and is exactly the way we approach the ministry to the Isaan people.

Churches can be planted in the most unpromising soil, be it Isaan Thailand or New Zealand. But it will only happen if we do our part of *the Great Commission partnership*, proclaiming the Cross and the Kingdom. If we do that, God will always act. He must! And that has been our experience in the various villages where we have planted churches. *He will do his 'bit' if we do our 'bit' FIRST.* Therefore, planning and strategy very much play an important part in bringing some guidelines to the way the ministry develops.

William Carey's 'Five Mission Principles' broadly align with what we tried to practice in Northeast Thailand:

1) Widespread preaching of the gospel (use every method).
2) Bible distribution (in local language).
3) Study the system of beliefs and thinking of the people.
4) Establish churches as quickly as possible.
5) Train local people for ministry as soon as possible.

Our experiences of ministry keys

In the next chapters, we will share some key strategies we found worked in our ministry to rural Isaan people. We are not suggesting these are the only keys, or in fact suitable in all situations, but share them here as an example of how God can reveal the best ministry approach for the situation the worker is in. These could be general principles that will apply in most rural Isaan villages but should be prayerfully considered.

In Acts 17:23, the Apostle Paul, while visiting Athens, walked around the city, observed, considered and saw a key entry point for the gospel in the shrine dedicated to 'an unknown god.' He brought a message to the Athenians from the 'unknown to them' God.

Seek the Lord to find your own keys, but what follows from our experiences may help.

Seven keys to reaching Isaan Village Buddhists

1) *Understand and embrace the social/cultural dynamics*
We need to think of the people we seek to reach in their social/cultural context. Effective evangelism in rural Thai villages is very different to what might be effective evangelism in the city. Villages are very different to the city, and socially they work in different ways. The greatest difference in villages is that people know each other and are frequently related.

Thai people living in cities often don't know their neighbours very well, or at all. This is particularly true of the new urban housing estates that have popped up all over Thailand, which copy residential developments in the 'West'. The residents drive to work and rarely talk to their neighbours, so these housing estates don't function like a real Thai village. We know this as we use to live in one of these urban 'mu baan' (villages).

But it's different in the rural villages, where traditional life is more preserved. We quickly noticed that village people not only knew their neighbours but their neighbour's business as well!

Frequently we would ask one of our village friends, 'where is so and so today?' They always had the answer! They always knew where they were and what they were doing. Living in a Thai village is like living in a goldfish bowl. The neighbours know everything you do and where you go.

Consider now the effect that will have on those attending a village church meeting. Everyone in the village will know you are attending a Christian meeting; so very early on, a 'seeker' will bear in mind that their neighbours will find out. That might be enough to scare some off.

We discovered after some time that Isaan villages were divided into sectors. If you were just visiting a village, you wouldn't pick this up, but the village may have several administrative sectors. There will be a leader for each sector, who reports to the Village Head, the Phuyaibaan.

What tends to happen in village life is that the residents of each sector work with each other on community events like tidying up the village or making things for the village temple. That will mean people will know best those who live in the same sector of the village. Other village people they may know only casually. What is also apparent is that over generations, the people of the sector are highly related. A son will build a house on his parent's land next to their house. Then their children build a house next door. Over time, the neighbourhood is made up of relatives.

Consider now if you tried to plant a church, meeting at someone's house at the northern end of the village. You then went all over the village sharing the gospel and inviting the interested to attend a meeting at this particular house. Who would come? Very likely only the invited people who lived in that same sector. In our early village work, we were mystified why people who seemed interested in finding out more about Jesus never came to a meeting at a particular house. We later understood that they lived in another sector of the village, and so were not familiar with the owner of the house and were not comfortable with coming.

Waew, coming from an Isaan urban dwelling family, didn't originally understand this either.

When we realised this dynamic, we targeted sectors within villages rather than trying to reach everyone in the village. In fact, several times in the early years we exhausted ourselves visiting an entire village door to door each week. When we succeeded in beginning a seeker church meeting at one believer's house, we quickly noticed the people who came were almost always only the direct neighbours. And those neighbours were actually relatives, cousins, in-laws and friends.

What we then tried was focused evangelism on just one sector of the village, the strategy being that it was potentially more efficient to work among people who were relationally connected. We had discovered that the gospel moved easiest along relational links in a chain, among friends and relatives. Stranger to stranger transfer of the gospel might start a gospel chain, such as in the case of the visiting Christian worker to a target village, but subsequent growth was almost always based on relationship links.

Another aspect of cultural context is something we noticed with the Thai National Church denominations. Thailand is a country that merges at least four distinct cultural groups; Northern Thai, Central or Bangkok Thai, Southern Thai and Northeast (Isaan) Thai. Each of these regions have their own language, which varies in degrees from Bangkok Thai which is the national language. Missionaries first translated the Bible into Bangkok Thai, and the churches they founded have used Bangkok Thai throughout the country as the language spoken in church meetings and used in publications. No doubt there were good logistical reasons, but when you learn the history of how the Thai Government in the past has tried to suppress the regional cultures in favour of a national identity, this ignoring of local culture by the Church was probably a mistake.

When visiting a city church in Northeast Thailand, we noticed the church members outside chatting in the local Isaan language, but when they went inside the church building and the service began, the pastor spoke in Bangkok Thai, even though he was an Isaan-born person. One Christian told us they felt like the 'Isaan' language was a 'low' language and not suitable for the dignity of a church meeting. Whether this idea was taught or came about by misunderstanding, it could be a stumbling block to reaching the Buddhist community. I recall the surprise I felt when a visitor to a city church said that they could not understand much of the vocabulary used in the city church meeting they attended. Because of this, we determined to use Isaan language in any meeting we held and use the local language when sharing the gospel in the streets as well.

Mission's organisations have recently picked up on embracing the local language, but the city churches still lag behind in this understanding. The Bible had only just been published in Isaan language when we returned to New Zealand in 2019. We believe greater success in reaching the Isaan people will come if the church was to embrace 'Isaan-ness' in its cultural expression of Christianity.

2) *Build relationships before introducing the gospel message*
Reaching village people with the gospel is all about relationships. Waew says it like this: 'Village people want to know you first. Then they will listen to your message.' In other words, we need to put relationships before the message. If the Thai church (and missionaries) have made a mistake in the last century, it is probably that they have put the message (gospel) ahead of building relationships with people. But that takes a commitment of time.

It is very interesting watching Waew interact with new people and the questions the villagers ask: 'Who are you? Where do you live? Where were you born? Where do your family live?' These are genealogy questions. They want to know her 'whakapapa' (family roots and ancestry), as Māori people would too. That's the introduction. Next, they ask you to eat food with them.

Waew says that sharing food is like becoming a member of the family. Now you are accepted, but you still have to build trust before they will listen to your message.

One day at a Wednesday morning church meeting at Nong Ping village, a woman passed by the gateway, and we invited her to join us. She had never been to the church meeting before, and carrying a plastic bag, it appeared she had just been to the market. But on prompting, she came in and sat in a vacant chair. Around her were 15 or 16 men and women who were her neighbours, friends, and undoubtedly some relatives. I reflected on how the gospel's path is smoothest where it passes through these established relationships. We can see people come to Christ through 'stranger to stranger' interaction, but it is harder. Our new friend stayed for the whole meeting. She was immediately comfortable with the people around her; they had known each other for years. This was a safe place.

Success in growing churches, particularly in rural villages, requires time spent building relationships. Thailand's villages receive visits from strangers every day, who stop and usually attempt to sell something. It's so prevalent that the average Thai villager is jaded and suspicious of any new face that turns up outside their house. Handing out a tract to this person or even a Bible is most likely not going to see fruit. Dozens of earlier travelling salesmen and even conmen have all been before. This is the barrier the gospel presentation faces.

Every missionary wants quick results. There's a need to write that monthly newsletter to the supporters back home, and they are all praying for results. That's probably why CPM is so attractive; it gives the promise of both speed and exciting statistics.

But what we noticed in the history of evangelism in Thailand and what we observed with city churches was a relatively small amount of time devoted to being a witness for Jesus. Typically, this meant a one-day visit to a rural village or using invitations to church neighbours to attend a Christmas celebration at the church. None of these methods focused on developing a relationship with the unsaved person.

Mass evangelism events typically failed, as those who responded on the day were not adequately followed up and discipled. What we observed in rural villages was that the village people were reserved and standoffish during our first visit to a village. We realised early on that we had to be committed to visit a village every week for at least six months. Someone might come to faith earlier, but experience showed most did not. It was during that six months that the village got to know us, and we got to know them. They learnt we were not wanting their money, and what we gave was for free. They learnt that we were trustworthy people, and we gained that trust by building relationships. In essence, we became friends.

In the early stages of visiting a village, we would focus on building that rapport with people, usually in a house-to-house walk. Waew loved talking to groups of people, and when we saw a group sitting outside a house, we would stop to introduce ourselves. Often, we would leave a gospel tract we had written with people. Willingness to receive a tract would soon indicate which people are more open. The following week we would refer to the tract previously given and ask people what they thought. It was then, with that feedback, that we got an indication if God was opening their hearts.

We heard some remarkable stories about how the written tracts had blessed people. Some old people had their grandchildren read it to them. That then communicated the gospel to another generation. Many times, we heard people saying how excited they were to receive the words of Jesus that they kept the tracts to read again and again under their pillow and literally 'slept on the Word.'

So, as this weekly visitation continued, the people we visited began to sort themselves based on openness and response to the message. After a couple of months, it was clear which people we visited were not at all interested in the 'good news.' Those not interested, we visited less frequently or stopped visiting, so we could spend more time with those who were 'seekers'.

What we saw next was people who were starting to develop a faith in Jesus. They started to tell us of dreams of Jesus and of prayers answered. At this point, we started thinking about where we could begin a meeting in the village. The answer was usually obvious, and it was just a matter of asking that person if they would host a meeting.

At this point we were at the cusp of seeing a church planted, but initially our approach would be to make an invitation to all those who we had visited over the preceding months to attend an inaugural meeting at a house. Sometimes we used community sala (an open-sided structure with a roof, common in villages), but this could lead to problems with other users at times. Out of the people invited to attend, the ones that came were usually who we expected would come. And this became the first seeker group.

The approach then changed focus from 'mobile' evangelism to teaching in one location. This can bring both advantages and disadvantages, but it is the most time effective as we spent our time with people who were genuinely interested. The weekly village visit remained, but the ministry becomes focused on a smaller group.

3) *From seeker group to a church that feels familiar*
In these Northeast Thailand rural villages, we would begin a 'seeker group' about six months after beginning our weekly visits to the village. Sometimes it happened faster; other times it was nine months before we began a meeting at one place in the village. Flexibility and the guidance of the Holy Spirit are key. Every village is different in terms of the spiritual climate and the level of stronghold Satan has in the village.

There were some villages we had to walk away from in the end, due to opposition. In one village, the Abbot had warned people about us and told them not to attend the seeker group we had just begun. We began a seeker group at a woman's house, and it went well, but the following week the atmosphere had changed, and she didn't want us to come to her house. Criticism from someone, either family, temple or neighbours is the usual reason. Someone else then opened their home and it went well for a month, then one week we arrived, and no one came.

In another village something similar happened. Things were going well at the meeting but, at the end, the woman who had appeared to be the 'person of peace' announced she didn't want to be involved anymore. Her grandson was a monk at the village temple, so we could imagine what might have happened. We thereafter met at a village sala, but the circumstances were not great and so we prayed another seeker would offer their house. The following week, another woman, Mae Min, offered her house, and the meeting quickly grew from seven to 15 people attending weekly. In every regard it was a better situation to plant a church.

Getting to the seeker meeting stage was not as difficult as we had been led to believe. We had heard stories of how resistant Thai people were to the gospel, and the lack of Christians doing what we were attempting tended to suggest that getting any sort of believer group going would be unlikely. However, as we tried just to walk by faith and believe Jesus' words, we saw success in about 70% of the villages we targeted. While in some villages we visited we were not able to begin a seeker meeting or plant a church, we found seven out of ten unreached villages could see a church planted given time, prayer, witness and diligence.

That is a statistic that is unknown with the traditional Thai church and missionary outreach approach. Our experience was that Thai people are not, as a group, closed to the gospel. The majority may be, but in every village there will be people whose heart the Holy Spirit will open and they will become disciples of Jesus. It may only be ten people, but if you seek them, you will find them with God's help.

When beginning our seeker meetings, the plan was to build on the awakened foundation of faith a person has. We discovered a discipleship resource produced by Overseas Missionary Fellowship (OMF) in Thailand and used this as a framework to disciple ten or a dozen people as a group.

Early after arriving in Thailand, we had a strong sense of what a village church should look like. We had visited churches in the urban areas, which had usually been started by a foreign missionary. There were local versions of the Catholic, Anglican, Presbyterian, Baptist, and Assembly of God churches. They were modelled in both their building architecture and meeting programme on churches in America and Europe. The church building was rarely recognisable as a Thai building, and invariably inside, people sat on pews or rows of chairs like in a Western church. But we thought, why shouldn't Thai church buildings look like a local design?

The meetings of these city churches were also Westernised. Worship songs in many Protestant churches seemed to be Hillsong translated into Thai, with music supplied by electric guitars, keyboards, and drum sets. Others used hymns and songbooks. Could any of this work in a rural village? We had our doubts.

We came to the conclusion that if we planted a church, we wanted the meeting of believers to feel normal and not foreign. We wanted to transfer faith in Jesus, not Western cultural expressions. In fact, a building was low priority as we intended to meet at people's homes in the same way the early Church also met in people's homes (see Acts). If the church grew, division into more house churches seemed preferable to building in bricks in mortar. As mentioned, we had seen problems in city churches with a designated church building becoming the home of the pastor's family as well. But ultimately, that was a decision for the village Christians to decide and beyond the scope of our time in ministry.

So we tried as much as possible for church meetings in the villages where we worked to feel normal to those who attended and to those who observed from the roadside. We sometimes met in a 'sala,' the traditional Thai structure with a roof and open sides, often located by a road for sheltering from rain or sun. These tended to be regarded as a public space where all were welcome. In other villages we met at a house, but usually outside. Thai people rarely invite non-family into their house. They are more comfortable entertaining guests outside under the shade of a roof. Often, we sat on the ground (concrete usually) on mats, with people in a circle as they would when eating food. Other times, as a church grew, it had to change to fit in more people, and we used plastic stacker chairs. The model was flexible and changed as needs changed. We also sought out worship songs written by Isaan Christians using traditional music and often accompanied with local traditional instruments which church members would play.

4) *Scripture distribution: Begin at the beginning*
We discovered there were good Thai language Christian teaching resources available through many mission agencies in Thailand, but it was necessary to carefully choose what material to use.

Buddhism has no creation story. This is an advantage for the Christian worker as the Genesis story gives a foundation for how life came about and an explanation of the origin of sin. Buddhism is silent on the origin of sin ('baap') or where life came from. Realising they were at a disadvantage to the Christians, the Buddhist monks in recent times have adopted evolution as their explanation of life.

Our experience in talking with village Buddhists was that they were more likely to accept the Biblical creation story than an evolutionary explanation, and so the teaching materials we used with new seeker groups would start at Genesis chapter 1, with the creation of life, the first man and woman, the Fall and introduction of sin to humanity, and the problem of sin in causing separation from God.

The reaction from the seekers to hearing this teaching was always positive. Some said they had heard this story before but couldn't be sure where. Others suggested the temple monks used to teach something similar many years ago about a creator God. These may be memories of a pre-Buddhist tradition that points to the coming of Jesus and will be discussed in a later chapter.

Having established an understanding of the origin of life and how sin came about, the next teaching would be on God's early involvement with the nation of Israel and the coming of Jesus the Saviour.

What we noticed is that when the seekers had come to a series of weekly meetings following this outline, by the time we started on the coming of Jesus, the people were ready to receive the Good News. A foundation was needed to enable understanding of why a saviour was needed. A mistake made by earlier missionaries and even some short-term workers today is to begin at Jesus and expect people will understand. They don't. Without an awareness of God as the Creator and an understanding of where sin came from, they will never understand who Jesus is. A clever chap called Engels worked out a scale that relates to a person's understanding of God and position on the path to faith and salvation.

The Engels Scale

- -7 No awareness of Christ
- -6 Aware of the existence of Christ (i.e., Muslims)
- -5 Have some knowledge of the gospel
- -4 Understanding of the fundamentals of the gospel: repentance, faith, the Cross
- -3 Aware of the personal implications
- -2 Recognition of a personal need
- -1 Challenged to receive Christ as Saviour and Lord
- 0 **Conversion/Salvation occurs**
- +1 Evaluation of the decision
- +2 Recognises and incorporated into the Body of Christ
- +3 Recognises his/her responsibility to communicate their faith to others

The Engels Scale helps us to understand where the people we meet are at. Thai Buddhists we met in villages were mostly at -7, with 'no awareness of Christ.' The role of the Christian worker and what we did in village evangelism was to gently prod them along that scale.

By the time we invite people to a seeker meeting, they will be at about -5 or -4, with a few at -2, but that is after at least six months of relationship building and teaching.

The mistake some Christian workers make with Thai Buddhists is shortly after meeting them, usually the same day, presenting a -1 challenge to receive Christ as Saviour. The person they are talking to, however, is still at -7 or -6 and so is not ready to receive

Jesus as Saviour. The evangelism effort ends with disappointment. Though a sinner's prayer was prayed, the Thai person didn't really understand (or was doing it to please you) and will likely fall away, 'seed sown on the path.'

Every person we meet is somewhere on this scale. What Christian workers need to do is to try and shift that person to at least the next step. One step at a time.

So, the important thing in working in these Thai villages is to understand that the journey of faith will take time for the future follower of Jesus. The Engels Scale can sometimes be short-circuited (such as when a divine healing occurs, and we've seen this), but for most who eventually become true Christians, there is a need to pass through the seven stages to salvation. The seeker groups move people along the Engels Scale, starting from around -5, then through to salvation, when the seeker group becomes the church in that village. We then stay with them, continuing to teach them into +1 to +3, where they finally understand their role and responsibility to share their faith with others. In our experience, this whole process for many people might take a year, perhaps longer for some.

The problem we see with those attempting a CPM approach with Thai Buddhists is they will attempt to move new contacts through the entire Engels Scale in a matter of days or weeks. This is not impossible but would require a particularly strong move of God in that person's life to occur and would be the exception rather than the rule from our experience to date.

Quite often a comment we heard at village meetings was, 'Now I understand!' As we continued to repeat doctrinal truth at each meeting, the person would have been someone who had heard the gospel many times since our early contact during a visit to their house or in a tract we had left with them. Yet it was not until months and months later that the 'penny dropped.' It used to remind us that these people are coming out of a spiritual fog. As Paul wrote, 'the god of this age has blinded the minds of the unbelievers' (2 Corinthians 4:4). What we discovered is the full escape from the fog of misunderstanding can take a long time of being exposed to the truth. And Satan will fight tooth and nail to hold onto those in the Kingdom of Darkness.

The Engels Scale also reminds us that the ultimate goal of seeing a believer change into a disciple of Christ involves stages of understanding and commitment by that person. There are many layers of revelation a person goes through before they are at that +3 level – 'recognising his/her responsibility to communicate their faith to others.' And then the battle begins within as to whether they will be obedient to that understanding.

5) Only the Holy Spirit can draw someone

After the seed has been sown, we know that for some it can lead to salvation, but the process of salvation is entirely the work of the Holy Spirit. Some people come to faith and commitment quickly, for others it takes longer, or they may fall away. Probably the most liberating revelation we received was that it was not our ministry but God's. And that it was not our words or actions that would see these village people receive Jesus as their Saviour, but the work of the Holy Spirit in their lives in various ways. In understanding this, it removed the burden of results from our shoulders and the expectation to see certain results within certain time frames. These were never burdens the Lord intended his servant workers to carry. Viewed from this perspective, success is not a certain number of salvations, baptisms and churches planted, but is obedience to what God has called the worker to do.

At this point, it is worthwhile to emphasise the importance of Jesus' parable of 'the sower,' or more correctly, the 'Parable of the Soils.' This parable clearly reveals there are four possible outcomes to every instance where the gospel has been preached to a person. Those working among Thai village people will experience the full spectrum of results as indicated in this parable. We cannot know beforehand whether a person has a 'good soil heart' that will result in them growing into a fruitful Christian, but we must treat every contact as if they do and will.

There are a variety of ways the Holy Spirit can draw someone to Christ, and we cannot predict how the Spirit will work other than what scripture teaches us. For example, John 16:8 states, 'When he comes, he will convict the world of guilt in regard to sin and righteousness and judgement.' The Apostle Paul seemed to be aware of this verse in Acts 24:25 when he spoke to Felix. Certainly, as we preach the gospel, the Holy Spirit is anointing the Word and working in hearts that hear. In fact, the only time we can be 100% confident that what we say will be anointed by the Spirit is when we are preaching 'Jesus Christ and Him crucified' and the related issues of sin, righteousness and future judgement by God.

The Spirit does work in other surprising ways, and one of these is dreams. Talk to most pastors in the Western church about dreams and you will be cautioned not to take much notice of them or of the possibility of being led astray if you are influenced to do something that you saw in a dream. Western churches would generally play down the likelihood that God might talk to us in a dream. This is despite the Bible being full of examples of God doing just that. But then, those were important people, we think to ourselves.

In Western culture, dreams are not generally regarded as having any significance, either in the church or in the secular world; however, the situation in Thailand is quite different. Thai people have a strong belief that dreams do have significance and relate to something important in their lives. Waew knew this, and I was surprised when we first married how often she talked about dreams and wondered what they meant. This is common with Thai people. They believe a dream is not just random entertainment for the subconscious.

When we began ministry in the villages and were praying for God to move in the lives of the people we were meeting, we started to meet some who had interesting dreams. At one village, we had been witnessing to an old man for several months, and he liked to read the Bible. Paw Bai told us one day in the previous week he had been reading his Bible before going to bed. That night, he had a dream where he saw himself seated and eating sticky rice and Isaan food with a 'holy man.' But there was something different. The holy man wore white robes, not the orange of the Buddhist monks, and why wasn't his face and head not shaved like a monk?

When he told us, we said, 'That sounds like Jesus!' Interestingly, we hadn't previously described to him what Jesus' appearance might look like, nor had we shown him any artist's pictures of the Lord. But the Lord did say in Revelation 3:20 that he would 'come in and eat with us.'

The following week, before going out to the village, I was reminded of this dream and found a tract that had a picture of Jesus on the cover. When we visited Paw Bai, I handed him the tract without comment. He took one look at it and said, 'That's the man!'

At another village, a woman who was a church member called Mae Dee had been feeling physically and spiritually weak for two days. For some time before, she hadn't been thinking much about the Lord and had neglected her prayer times. For two days she felt so weak that she couldn't rise off her bed, and she really thought she was going to die. She even told her son about the funeral arrangements. What was going on?

On the second night, she had a dream in which she saw two shining figures. They came to her and said, 'You are already going the right way, pray to God!' When she awoke, she immediately prayed to the Lord and prayed in the Spirit. She then opened her Bible and read, and soon after felt her strength return so she was able to get up and go about her work as normal. Talking to Mae Dee later, we told her she probably was under attack from Satan but having neglected her quiet times with God and Bible readings had opened her to an attack from the enemy.

Our message is not Christ versus Buddha. A mistake a Christian worker can make with Folk Buddhists is being too eager to push them over the 'salvation line.' It might look good if you are counting salvations for a monthly report, but that really is not the way to draw people to Christ. In fact, it is God who draws in the sinner: 'But I when I am lifted up from the earth, will draw all men to myself' (John 12:32).

In that early stage of the seeker, we were careful not to be too confronting in the message we gave people. We are not preaching a Jesus versus Buddha message. Buddhists have great respect for their religion and figures in their religion like the Buddha. Any words of criticism towards the Buddha or Buddhism will immediately cause a Thai to close their mind and reject the message without further consideration.

If a missionary was to tell a Thai their religion was invented by Satan and the Buddha was deceived by a demon, they would be deeply insulted and close their mind to any further discussion. One time, Waew was asked to translate for a visiting outreach team from a Western country. At a rural village, the team leader began preaching to a crowd of locals. As he began his discourse, Waew was alarmed at the confrontational approach of his gospel message. Thinking, 'I can't say this,' she modified and toned down the message, removing any insulting references to Buddha being deceived by Satan and focused instead on what Jesus did. The message was well received, and the team, completely unaware there had been some slight change, were happy with the friendly response.

Some Christian workers would tell a new salvation-seeker very early in witnessing that 'if you become a Christian, you must stop visiting the temple' – a requirement that seemed to be justified as part of 'counting the cost.' But this approach will turn many away before they have even considered the claims of Jesus. Many will be saved and become fully committed to Christ if this aspect of the social/cultural connection to the temple is left until later in the journey of faith in Jesus. We found that we didn't need to tell people to stop attending temple ceremonies and festivals. The believers would make that decision themselves and reach the realisation by the conviction of the Holy Spirit. The Spirit would Himself tell them they didn't need the temple anymore. And they would then tell us.

Our message when speaking to Isaan people was to talk about Jesus, who He is and what He did. We avoided comparing Christianity to Buddhism and never criticised the Buddha or his teaching. There is no need. By speaking the words of Jesus, the truth is anointed by the Holy Spirit, and the listener will hear what God wants them to hear. They will in time receive the revelation that they don't need to hang onto the old ways when they receive new life in Christ. Confronting people with what seems like an attack on their beliefs builds a wall rather than a bridge to God. If we allow the words of Jesus to do their work in the lives of people, the Spirit will 'draw' that person in a gentle, non-confrontational way. Thai culture is to avoid confrontation where possible, and this approach is the most culturally sensitive and ultimately will result in far more people giving the gospel a hearing.

6) *Tell them Jesus is more powerful than the spirits*
'The reason the Son of God appeared was to destroy the devil's work.' (1 John 3:8)

Most Buddhists realise they can't follow all the teaching and rules of the Buddhist religion, which would require someone to become a full-time monk and devote their lives to meditation. Incidentally, women miss out badly in Buddhism, but that's another story.

So, ordinary Buddhists try to keep the minimum precepts and gain merit by doing good deeds, such as feeding the monks and giving temple donations. But life's problems and challenges have to be overcome some way, and for this, the Folk Buddhist relies on a legion of spirits and gods who they hope will help if they are served in some way.

In every city, town and village in Northeast Thailand, shrines honouring these deities can be seen. They are worshipped with gifts, flowers, dances and offerings. The people will use fortune-tellers, who are in touch with the spirits, to guide every major decision in life. They wear amulets around their necks and have special tattoos to give them protection, health and success.

Young children can be dedicated to a particular spirit. Shops have shrines to ensure business is good. Many houses will have a spirit house outside where the resident spirit is appeased and hopefully kept out of the home. Although these little structures are picturesque in tourism photos, the reality is that the spirits are not the people's friends.

It is staggering the extent of idolatry, occult practices and spirit worship that goes on in Thailand, and it can appear impregnable. But the Bible tells us we have weapons that have divine power to demolish strongholds.

In one village we worked in, many people lived in fear of wandering ghosts, or 'Phee,' who they believe kidnap people, usually children, at night. These folk wouldn't go outside at night, and they made a scarecrow figure at their gateway to scare off the Phee.

Imagine going to bed knowing that your dreams will likely be dark nightmares where you are pursued by snakes, demons and ghosts. This is a normal occurrence for most Thai Buddhists, as Waew can testify was her experience before she met Jesus. The more that the spirit beings are worshipped it seems the more it opens the door to nocturnal dream-time attacks from Satan's hordes.

A lady called Mae Som Peun was just one of many who told us since becoming a follower of Jesus, nightmares and bad dreams had ended. Satan's access to the Christian's subconscious is shut down.

Paul tells us in Ephesians 6:12, 'For our struggle is not against flesh and blood, but against the rulers, against the authorities, against the powers of this dark world and against the spiritual forces of evil in the heavenly realms.'

Living in a Western secular country, it could be easy to doubt the existence of such beings, but spend some time in Thailand, talk to the people and observe, and soon you will realise they do exist, and they are constantly on people's minds. And this really is the key with Folk Buddhism. Spirit worship/appeasement is about how to navigate life today and solve today's problems and needs, which is something Buddhism, in its true form, has no answer for.

Here, of course, is the opening for the gospel, as Buddhism fails in this basic need of being useful to life in the here and now, and spirit worship and the occult only opens the door to malevolent powers. It's interesting that in the gospel accounts of Jesus' ministry, we see immediate action by Jesus against the hold of evil spirits. In fact, the number of encounters Jesus had with demons is surprising, many occurring while visiting the synagogue.

Frequently, Jesus himself accounts for an illness as being the work of a demon: 'Then should not this woman, a daughter of Abraham, whom Satan has kept bound for 18 long years, be set free on the Sabbath day from what bound her?' (Luke 13:16). Or a few verses later in verse 32, 'Go tell that fox (Herod), I will drive out demons and heal people today and tomorrow, and on the third day I will reach my goal.'

Jesus' earthly ministry contained the challenge to repent and believe the Good News, while also engaging Satan in a counterattack that turned the tables in what Satan's rule on earth involved. Jesus commissioned his disciples to do likewise: to go into all the world and preach the good news, drive out demons and lay hands on sick people so they are healed.

So, in bringing the gospel to rural people in villages in the Isaan region, we should be covering all aspects Jesus outlined in the Great Commission, including looking for opportunities to bring healing and release from those under the power of Satan.

We prayed for healing for people at every church or seeker meeting and saw many healed over the years. We had a few encounters with demonic powers during that time as well. In one village, there was a village madman who lived near where we met at a house for a church meeting. He often shouted, screamed and cried out but always seemed to leave his house and disappear for a time when we began to sing worship songs. Once I saw his face contort as he looked towards me, and in that second I saw a different face leering at me, before it disappeared just as quickly, the face of the demon controlling this man.

At the same village one day, Waew was visiting a believer, Mae Dtoom, and went with her to another house where a relative of Mae Dtoom, a man called Jaan, lived. As they entered the house calling out for Mr Jaan, they heard a commotion coming from the bathroom. Jaan soon emerged, shaking uncontrollably with spasms and shouting for people to leave him alone. Waew noticed that he wouldn't look at her and immediately discerned this was a demonic manifestation. While Jaan's sons had run off in fear, Waew and Mae Dtoom managed to move him to a bed. And all the time he was shaking and flailing around uncontrollably and avoiding Waew's eyes.

Waew told Mae Dtoom to 'start praying!' as they tried to hold him down. Then confidently, Waew commanded the evil spirit to 'leave in Jesus' name!' The moment she spoke, 'In Jesus' name!' the shaking stopped, and he was at peace. Mae Dtoom was wide-eyed in amazement at the power and authority of the name of Jesus.

At the seeker and church meetings, we would frequently teach on the authority of the believer, the power of the name of Jesus, and that Jesus had come to destroy the devil's work. We told people that as children of God they no longer needed to be afraid of ghosts, Phee and evil spirits. We don't worship or appease them. We drive them out in the name of Jesus. This message was met with great relief and excitement.

This aspect of the Gospel message is vitally important and will result in the new believers developing as Kingdom-of-God-building disciples in their community.

7) *Saved from sin by grace, not by works*

In Thailand, it is never difficult or awkward to have a conversation with a Buddhist person on spiritual matters and religion. This surely must be the most obvious difference with evangelism in Thailand compared to New Zealand (or other Western 'Christian' nations). The reason for this is almost everyone has spiritual and religious beliefs. You find very few atheists in Thailand. Discussing matters of religion in Thailand is as normal as discussing the weather. People will listen respectfully and rarely take offence. However, simply because they listen doesn't mean they will understand or believe what we say. But we continue sowing that seed in the belief that the Holy Spirit can germinate the revelation of truth in lives.

Francis Xavier didn't regard Buddhism as a religion as it taught no creation story or supreme God. Once we understand Buddhism is a works-based ideology, we can meet it at the point that ordinary adherents can understand, and that is the problem of sin and how to deal with it. In Buddhism, there is a strong belief in sin (bad or wrong actions) and that there are consequences for that. Buddhists do recognise moral failures and how actions affect our eternal destiny. This is the idea of karma, simplified as 'do good, receive good. Do bad receive bad.'

Thai Buddhists also believe in a place similar to hell called Narok. Just when a sinner might get there is a little vague, but presumably after numerous reincarnations of a descending order, eventually the incorrigible sinner hits the rock bottom of Narok. The idea of a hell-like place is well-formed in Buddhist minds. In temples, there are often fiery murals depicting the unfortunates who are in Narok, with demons torturing them. These pictures are designed to terrify the Buddhist to stay on the Buddha's pathway. In some ways these do resemble paintings by various Medieval European artists, so the consequences of sin are well understood by the Buddhist.

If we are in a conversation with a Thai Buddhist and we mention Romans 3:23, 'For all have sinned and fall short of the glory of God,' they will agree with us. If we move onto Romans 6:23, 'For the wages of sin is death...,' they will also agree with us, saying, 'We have the same teaching!' But it is when we move on to Ephesians 2:8-9 that the stark difference between Buddhist teaching and Christianity is brought into sharp focus.

Paul writes, 'For it is by grace you have been saved, through faith... not by works, so that no one can boast.' Buddhism relies on the self-effort of doing good works to pay the penalty of sin. And they have a confidence their method will work. Christianity undermines that boasting confidence by clearly stating on the authority of the Bible that sin can only be paid for by God's grace for those who, by faith, receive the free gift of the Saviour's work. Jesus' work did it once and for all.

Buddhism holds up the need for never-ending work by the individual to counter sin accumulated in a person's life. The Bible teaches us it cannot be done by human effort. The good news really is Jesus has already done the work for each individual who believes by faith. Here is the key point in evangelism of Buddhists – if they grasp that their self-effort at 'goodness' is doomed to failure and that the years of 'tham boon' (making merit) will not deal with their sin, they will gratefully embrace the freedom and grace available by the Saviour Jesus' death on the Cross.

In a sense, our message doesn't contradict the Buddhist's concern about sin, but rather reveals to them the solution they never knew about. And many older Isaan people have an inkling that there is a better way to come, which relates to the oral prophecy of the coming of Phra See Ahn. This will be covered further in chapter seven.

CHAPTER 5

Keys We Discovered for Starting a Seeker Meeting

We've noticed a few familiar occurrences around starting a new seeker meeting in a village. As mentioned already, we wouldn't usually attempt to begin a meeting until we had spent a least six months weekly visiting an unreached village. During that time, we developed friendships and relationships and shared portions of the gospel and the knowledge of God with these new friends. At some point, we would become aware of roughly how many people we think would be interested in joining a meeting where the stories of the Creator God and the Saviour Jesus are explained in greater detail.

When we thought at least ten people could come, we began the process of changing the ministry modus operandi from mobile and village-wide to a relatively fixed location. In other words, from a village-wide focus to the neighbourhood. Once gaining agreement from someone to host this meeting, we made an invitation, photocopied it and distributed it around the village, door to door. The invitation was for a meeting to begin the following week, all welcome.

At our first meeting, we would usually have all ladies, even though there were at least four or five men we knew were interested. But this is normal; the men are more nervous of criticism than the women. Men tend to hold positions in a village that could result in criticism if they came to a church meeting, especially if they may be on the village temple committee. We pray the men will join in later, but in the early stages they tend to send their wives!

The second week we might have a few less attending, but maybe a few more men. At one village, Mae Tuk told us rumours had gone out in the village about 'us.' The people have usually heard stories of what happens in some other villages where Christians collect people on Sunday and take them away to a secret meeting in the city. 'Who knows what goes on at those meetings!'

Now, none of this surprised us. It's just the Devil's standard scare tactic to keep people away from Christian meetings. We had anticipated this particular ploy, but it does highlight how the practice of 'Catch and Carry' (that most city-based churches use) can be counterproductive and do more harm than good. Our approach was always that every village needs a church. Don't take them away to that secret meeting, open a meeting at their house!

We can't overstate the importance of meetings being open and transparent in a village community. We held all the seeker meetings outside and in sight of neighbours and other village people. This way there was nothing secret, and everyone in the village could see for themselves what went on. This is important to gain tolerance and even acceptance from the Buddhist majority. In one village, the Temple Abbott would drive past our meeting every so often in his orange car to keep an eye on us and I guess take note of numbers attending. After several months of meetings, there should be a normality in the eyes of the other villagers about Christ believers meeting in the village.

One year on, we would see a small core of believers double in number, with the newer members coming from neighbouring houses. Many of these new people we would have met a year earlier when we trudged the streets, meeting and witnessing to people in the village, but they held off coming to any church meetings until a year had passed. Our church meeting, typically down a small lane, would now be a regular accepted weekly event in the community of that soi (lane). The neighbourhood children would come to the meeting when school was out and during school holidays. Even non-believing households sent their kids along to the church meeting. The neighbours felt comfortable to drop in. Why not, as the church members are their friends and family? Isn't church meant to be like this?

The curious and the hungry are ready to come. At Khok See village we planted a church, hosted in the home of a local woman named Mae Lek. Mae Lek told us of a friend who said to her, 'I go to the temple often and worship many gods, but I feel nothing. I would like to come to your group sometime to hear about your God.'

As the children and adults heartily sing the gospel Isaan songs, they are repeating gospel truths, and the Spirit works in those hearts, including those of young children who hear of this Saviour called Jesus. Change can come quickly for some, but for others, faith may not come, or it may come progressively as week by week they are exposed to the power of the Word of God. Other people will reach out to church members they know.

At this stage, those standoffish men are starting to soften. They do read all the handout material we give out at the meetings to their wives, and we know some will become believers as a result of their wives' testimonies and the written gospel material they have read. We visit houses of church members as well, and this is a great way to get to meet the husbands.

Structure is important to Thais

Getting people to come to a meeting is one thing, but equally important is what they hear and experience while there. It should be new but not necessarily presented in an unfamiliar way.

Looking at the Buddhist traditions and practices in villages, it was clear they were familiar with liturgy and some structure in a meeting. Thai people view things through their own cultural lens. The presentation should not distract from the message. I recall years earlier, while at university, I took along a Thai student to a New Zealand church service. It was a Pentecostal church with a lively preacher. Asking the student afterwards for their impression, they said the preacher for them seemed 'like a crazy man' with his jumping around and waving of his arms. For the student, the quiet, dignified behaviour of a Buddhist monk was a better model of a spiritual teacher.

When starting a house church in a village, we felt the meeting needed to have structure, as Thais like structure in a meeting programme. We wanted to have three elements in all meetings: prayer, worship, and Bible teaching, followed by prayer ministry where needs could be prayed for.

We decided we would use a structured liturgy approach, borrowing from the Anglican tradition, beginning the meeting with a Prayer of Confession. This seemed important as often we had unsaved new people at the meetings. It also would mean that people would learn the prayer by its repetition at each meeting. We would follow that with a time of worship, singing gospel and worship songs written by Thai and Isaan believers.

Usually after the worship, we would all recite the Apostles (Nicene) Creed together. Again, the use of the Creed every week meant those who came would learn it and all its doctrine. As new Christians, these folk had no earlier cultural understanding of Christianity, and so these structural elements were vital in causing the biblical truths to sink deep into their consciousness. The Creed, with its ancient origins in the Council of Nicaea, was also an opportunity for those there to reaffirm or declare their faith in

Jesus publicly. We would usually finish the meeting after the Bible teaching by praying the Lord's Prayer.

Structure and repetition were important to enable doctrine to be remembered. This can sometimes be overlooked by workers from a Christian family background. An important benefit of this approach is that it enables the believer to become a better witness of the gospel as they have memorised the doctrine of their Faith and can repeat it from memorised sections of the Creed during evangelism opportunities.

The ministry approach we used over a number of years changed to some extent as a result of what we learned in the various villages. As previously mentioned, at Nong Siang village we attempted to reach every household in the village, going house to house. It took a long time to get around, and while it was pleasing to expose an entire village to the gospel, we spread ourselves too thin. When it came to trying to gather seekers to a meeting to begin discipleship, the people themselves came from different parts of the village and many did not know each other. Is that a problem? Yes, it was an issue because in villages, people are most comfortable with the family and friends they live with. Going to a stranger's house for a meeting, even in their own village, was too daunting for many. People said they would come to the meeting but never did.

What we noticed was the ones who came to the meeting were from one soi (lane) and were relatives and friends. This confirmed something we had noticed in earlier church plants – that the gospel passed easiest along family networks and friendship webs. Stranger-to-stranger passage was rare. In fact, in the beginning, we were the strangers and we had to become friends before they would consider the gospel message. Think about that.

Later, when we began working at an unreached village, we decided not to attempt to reach the whole village ourselves but to target a subcommunity of friends and family. We knew that in villages, families built houses next to each other, so on any road or soi, you would find related people and friends who were neighbours. We began in a random block and intensively went house to house. As the area was smaller, we got to see the same people more often and had time to get to know them. When we invited people to a seeker meeting about six months later, people readily came.

Wives leading husbands to Christ

Back in 2010, a Christian organisation surveyed 3,000 church members in Thailand to uncover some of the features of conversion experiences from ex-Buddhists. One of the interesting findings was that most Buddhist husbands of Christian women do eventually become Christians themselves, although it can take up to ten years (1 Corinthians 7:14).

Another finding that emerged from the survey is that older Thai people (i.e., older than 60 years) are *twice* as likely to become Christians than teenagers aged between 15 and 19 years.

That finding runs counter to the popular idea that the young would be more open to the gospel than the old. And our observation was that the amount of ministry effort to reach the young in student outreaches was greater than those targeting the older generation. Certainly, working with older people in villages has shown us that the older generation is keenly aware of their sin and failings and a death that won't be too far off!

We often saw wives lead their husbands to Christ. Mae Paa is a bubbly woman in her sixties who had been a believer in Jesus for about six months. Her spiritual growth was ballistic. At meetings, she always had something to say about how God had blessed and changed her. She regularly brought unsaved friends to church meetings.

What we didn't realise was the effect she was having on her husband, Paw Garn, who we hadn't met. He was also affected by her transformation. At a church meeting one time, we were excited to see him come. He stood up and with tears in his eyes said, 'I know this is the true God. I have been unwell and had much pain in my eyes. I cried out to God to heal me, and he did.' Paw Garn went on the explain he had been a Buddhist Monk for 19 years, but now he was a follower of Jesus.

At Nuuw village, one of the ladies told us how her husband eagerly waited to read the weekly gospel handout sheets, with its portions of scripture, that we distributed at the church meeting. At night he lay on the bed, reading God's word. Though he had never come to the seeker meeting, he was a 'seeker' who was being reached through his wife's testimony and the power of the written Word of God. We noticed this happening in all the villages. The impact and reach of the village church meetings went beyond the believers who actually came, which of course is how it should be in all healthy churches.

Mae Gwaat had been a believer since early on in our ministry at her village, and she brought her sister along to hear the gospel. Soon they were both saved. Mae Sangwan told the church members one time how her husband had many health ailments. She would take home a weekly teaching tract and read it to her husband. At first, he wasn't interested, but as she continued week by week, he eagerly awaited her return from the church meeting. Next, she prayed for his healing in Jesus' name, and his health improved. Then, on one Monday, she was leaving home to attend the church meeting. Her husband asked her, 'Aren't you going to the temple today?' (It was an important Buddhist day.) She replied, 'No, I'm going to worship my God.' Her husband nodded. 'Up to you,' he said. This man also opened to the gospel through the witness of his wife. One of numerous cases we were aware of during our ministry time in Northeast Thailand.

The written word is still a key

It was incidents like this that alerted us to the real benefit of literature, handouts and tracts in ministry to Isaan villages. In recent years, some from mission's circles have poo-pooed the use of literature as 'old style' ministry compared with the use of oral stories and dramatic presentations of the gospel. Certainly, with people groups without a written language or working with the illiterate, that approach could well be best. But Thailand has a very high level of literacy. Ninety-year-old village great-grandmothers we met could read Thai. So why not use that avenue? And if you are trying to reach a friend or family member you haven't met, a printed message means the story is delivered in entirety and unchanged from what you, as the change agent, intend them to receive. There is no chance of a 'Chinese whispers' type corruption of the message from being incorrectly relayed in a story.

We prepared a handout each week to give to all who attended the seeker or church meetings. People could then take this home for other family members to read. The other benefit was the teaching going on at the meeting was then understood by other family, and that enabled some wives to continue coming, as their husbands had read and approved of our teaching.

We also strongly believe in the power of the Word of God and that in reading scripture, the Holy Spirit can confirm and convict the reader of truth. This powerful spiritual dimension was another reason we like to have believers taking home something in writing relating to the teaching message of that week.

One of the real challenges with regards to the Bible in Thailand is that, while readily available in the Thai language, it has only recently been translated into the Isaan language. During our time in Thailand, the Isaan New Testament was just becoming available. We obtained copies for all the village churches where we worked.

An early mistake of the mission organisations was to treat all regions of Thailand as if they were culturally 'Bangkok Thai.' They are not, and deserve their cultural differences to be expressed, such as the use of the local language in church meetings. Bible colleges tended to be staffed by missionary teachers who only spoke Central Thai, and so all teaching was done in the national language, which is the Bangkok dialect. This has become the language of use in church meetings and Bible translations, despite the fact that for much of the country it is not the local 'heart language.'

Thai Bibles, including the Isaan New Testament, are printed in a small font, presumably to make the book smaller and cheaper to produce. Unfortunately, this small font can be near impossible for elderly people to read. We had a great struggle trying to find a version of the Bible that wasn't in tiny print that our older people could read. The publishers seem to have forgotten this important fact. If the script is too small, only the young will be able to read it.

What about reading glasses? We tried that as well. In fact, for several years at Christmas we bought reading glasses for all the members of the village churches we had planted. That worked well for a while, but usually within six months they were broken, lost or lent to someone else. But this issue of being able to read the Word of God was too important to our thinking to give up, so we decided to print out scripture portions in a large font print size to give to church members.

Two of the goals of our ministry to the village churches was to see the saints become *people of prayer* and *people of the Word*. In this culture, the second goal can be difficult as while most people are literate, reading is limited in daily life to essentials; pill bottles, government notices etc. Reading for pleasure is uncommon in villages. Even newspapers are rarely seen. So, training people to daily read God's Word is a challenge. Over the years, we tried various Bible versions and eventually came up with *Bite-size Bible Bits*, a two-page, A4-sized chapter of the Bible (30-40 verses) that we gave out at the end of all meetings. The idea was for it to not be an intimidating 1,000-page volume your eyes can barely read. Villagers could sit down and read a chapter quickly and collect it together with others in a file folder for later referral, or to give away to an interested neighbour. It seemed to work well, and the people liked these 'manageable servings' of the Bible. More pure scripture was being read, and that's got to be healthy!

A very good teaching book aimed at village Christians was made available to us one year.

The book was produced by some missionary friends who were also working in Isaan villages, and they kindly sent us a digital file which we printed out and reproduced as a bound book of 35 pages, with a clear plastic front cover and cardboard back page. We printed 100 books for use in the village house churches and were very excited about this new tool. The book was very well received around all the churches, and many told us it helped them understand better than they did before.

The book, called *Follow me! The 10 Commands of Lord Jesus*, went through ten chapters entitled:

1) Repent and believe in Jesus
2) Receive the Holy Spirit
3) Baptise others
4) Practice Communion
5) Love God and others
6) Pray always

7) Give joyfully
8) Heal the sick, cast out demons and raise the dead
9) Take up your cross and be willing to suffer for Christ
10) Help others to follow Jesus too

These chapters were filled with gospel stories and parables and beautifully illustrated by a Thai artist using traditional Esarn Buddhist temple fresco style. A good example of a contextualised literature resource.

Later on, we produced a 27-page, A4-sized booklet for the village churches entitled *Worship God!* It gathered together prayers, worship songs, specific teachings and some key gospel-related scriptures, all in a large Thai script font so elderly people could read it, even without glasses. We produced 100 copies and distributed them around the village churches we were working with at the time.

CHAPTER 6

The Gospel Produces Fruit

By nature, Isaan people are compliant and eager to please. That means they can appear receptive or committed when they are not. Many a missionary has been fooled over the years by this cultural willingness to please. An example would be the overuse of a 'sinner's prayer' card. Thai people, unlike people in many Western countries, will willingly pray a 'sinner's prayer' if you ask them. The Thai would think, 'It can't hurt,' and they don't want to disappoint you after you spent ten minutes explaining your story about Jesus. We saw this happen many times; willing to pray a prayer but with no actual faith in Jesus.

Only the work of the Holy Spirit can truly save and transform a person. This sometimes happens quickly, but in our experience, it mostly takes a period of years for the last tentacle of Buddhism to fall away. Then they will follow their Lord through thick and thin and not just be 'Sunday Christians.' Here lies another reason the promise of the Church Planting Movements may fail to deliver.

We always wanted to see people grow in faith in Jesus, as we knew that if they lacked that strength of faith, they could easily return to Buddhism for one reason or another. We focused our ministry on two things: evangelism and disciple-making. The first stage with some people can be quite quick; the second stage (disciple-making) can take much longer. It is during that stage that the 'stony ground hearers of the Word' fall away. But the result for those who endure is real followers of Christ with real faith and, in time, fruit.

> '...all over the world this gospel is producing fruit and growing, just as it has been doing among you since the day you heard it and understood God's grace in all its truth.' (Colossians 1:6)

Notice Paul's key point regarding gospel growth: 'and understood God's grace in all its truth.' From our experience, the day a person 'hears' and the day a person understands, may not be the same day!

Knowledge about God can fill the head, but it must migrate lower to the heart. It is there it becomes faith. Knowledge without faith will not produce fruit and multiply. One of the frustrations of field workers is the home team wanting to know about the multiply part, but that is often a step beyond where an individual or church group is at. Seeing a foundation on Christ being firmly established in people that have come from a Buddhist background is not achieved in a day. It can take a long time. But we need that foundation first. Once established, fruit and growth will come.

Passing the baton; developing leaders

It almost goes without saying that one of the goals of the church planter is to develop leaders who can take over and allow the church planter to ease themselves out. We all know that missionaries should be working themselves out of a job. Hudson Taylor gave the memorable analogy of missionaries being the scaffolding around a rising building (the church) and said the sooner they can be dispensed with the better. The problem is what we all understand and agree with can be harder to achieve in practice than in theory. The saying, 'easier said than done,' comes to mind.

Every missions' situation is different, and with small groups of new believers, it can be difficult to find someone within the group who is both willing to step into leadership and undergo training. With any small group of ten to a dozen people, there could be a range of situations from several people with potential and who are willing, to none visible at all. This is equally true of church cell groups in the Western church.

From our first church plant village, we were prayerfully looking for new believers in the group who could develop as leaders and evangelists. In some cases, these people left to live in another town or city, some tragically died before they reached their potential, and others left the village and associated themselves with a city church.

In one village, a young woman seemed to have potential to lead. She had taught herself to play the guitar to make herself useful in ministry and seemed eager. We encouraged her, and when we returned home for three months, we asked her to lead the church meetings. This she did, and we had good reports, so we talked to her about taking on the leadership of the church meeting. For several weeks we gave her guidance and came along to support. She did well, including preparing for a Bible teaching lesson, so we passed the baton. Unfortunately, before long, we heard troubling reports. She was late to meetings, even though she lived in the village. She was unprepared for teaching even though she had a week to prepare. The other church members were not impressed. It may have been a little of the 'prophet without honour in their own village,' but there was an element of laziness. We suspected the young woman needed a job and the salary we paid fitted the bill. She didn't see this ministry as a calling; it was a job. After a while, we had to dispense with her services simply because she was not putting in the effort.

After that experience, we decided we would not pay people to lead church meetings but rather wait for people who God called and felt called by God to the ministry. The need for a job had to be a secondary consideration in the mind of the local person. They had to be doing it as service to God. With a person like this, we were happy to cover their costs so they could serve.

If it feels like a 'drop in the bucket,' make the bucket smaller!

In 2015, we began work in the village of Pia Faan. As villages go, it's on the small side, with 150 households and probably an adult population of 500 people. From no Christians, two years later there were about 20 believers and a few on the border. Not many perhaps, but as a percentage of the village adults, Pia Faan is much better off than most of Thailand, and better off than most of the Isaan region, where Christian witness averages about 0.1% of the population. And it's the same in all the villages we worked in. A dozen or so Christians can seem like a 'drop in the bucket' if you focus on the macro-need, but highly significant when viewed in a micro-community like a village.

In fact, a non-believer in one of our ministry villages is probably five times more likely to be touched by the gospel than someone living in Bangkok or another large city. Less really is more when it comes to magnifying the 'salt and light' of Christian witness! Particularly when you realise that village people are far more relational than people living in cities who may rarely speak to or know their neighbours. Village people actually talk to their neighbours.

One church in an Isaan village potentially has more influence than one in a city suburb as the population is so much smaller. And we saw this effect in each village we worked in. Once the church has been established for a year or two, it seems the fear of the timid types is overcome, and they will check out what the Christians are doing. And so we saw new people dropping in to join the church meeting each week. Sometimes they were invited by church members, other times they came by themselves. This is less common in the early stages of a new church when a lot of neighbours will wait and watch before daring to come to a meeting (Acts 5:13).

However, we had not noticed this happen much in the city churches we'd had some involvement with. Why is this? One of the reasons is surely that village people are more closely related by family, friendship and acquaintance. There is a greater likelihood the unsaved will know, hear or meet a Christian in a village where there is a church. In cities, this is less likely as the 'bucket' is so much bigger.

With this backdrop in mind, we developed our strategy of 'rings of righteousness.' The idea is to plant churches in neighbouring villages that link together like a chain and encircle a district. Imagine a circle of villages, each village a few kilometres apart, each with a church and praying Christians focused on their sub-district. Consider also the web of relationships with cousins and in-laws living in neighbouring villages.

We saw this occur in one district. Four villages formed an unbroken chain of Christian influence in a Buddhist hinterland. To the immediate north they meet two other villages, where our American friends, the Hughes, had planted two churches. So, the encirclement of the district is nearly complete. One village is still unreached, as we were unsuccessful in planting a church after a year of effort. But the influence in the district and the heavenlies above is significant.

Seeing God at work; fruit with perseverance

One day in January 2018, we headed out to Nong Ping village for a regular church meeting and found ourselves leading a funeral. The Nong Ping village church met at Mae Nu's house. She was one of the first believers in the village and was an elderly woman. As we arrived at the village, we immediately knew something had happened. A tent had been set up outside the house on the road frontage, people were milling around, and chairs were set out.

As we feared, Mae Nu had died the day before, and so this was the second day of the funeral. Funerals in Isaan start immediately after someone dies and can go on for four days. Mae Nu's adult daughter (also a church member) met us and explained the situation. We were not completely surprised, as Mae Nu had been unwell for six months, spending recent time in hospital. Most of the village people and neighbours had visited the day before.

Inside the house, Mae Nu's casket was there in an ice-packed cooler, and we prayed beside the casket as is traditionally done. We were thinking we would need to cancel the planned church meeting when the Puuyaibaan (village leader) said, 'You can preach now!' Over to the side, a circle of chairs was already set out and about a dozen of the believers were already seated and waiting.

Now, it just so happened that week in all the villages we had been teaching on judgement and eternal life from Revelation chapters 20 and 21. We agreed, 'Let's go with it.' What a text to preach at a funeral! We adapted the meeting into a Christian funeral for Mae Nu, and the topic of what the Bible says about final judgement and eternal life for believers was powerfully presented. The relevance of the message was lost on no one. In fact, on the other side of the front fence where the Christian funeral was taking place, a group of men gambled with dice. This is common at Buddhist funerals, so the contrast between sinners and saints was clear to all, and it turned into a great opportunity for the gospel.

Mae Nu's two sons and one of her daughters were at the meeting, as well as several other unsaved family members. All of these took away Christian reading material. Mae Nu was remembered as the woman of faith and child of God she was, and the family asked for the church to continue to meet at the house in the future. This we did, with Mae Nu's adult son saved and opening the house as a meeting place thereafter.

Go out of your way to sow seed into lives

In most villages, every little street has one or more small shops, convenience stores really, built in front of a house. They are open early and close late, with at least one member of the family on duty all day. We've met and witnessed to many shopkeepers in villages over the years but reaching them with the gospel is a challenge as they will usually not shut their shops to attend a church meeting. Business always seems to come first.

At one village, there was one of these shops opposite Mae Min's house, where the village church meets. We got to know the elderly woman who owned the shop, and she could hear and see the church meeting from her side of the soi. She seemed interested but would never come to the meeting, and so we left her one of our gospel literature tracts each week, which she received gladly. Church members who were her neighbours said she made comments to them that showed she was developing a faith in Jesus. This went on for all of 2018. We left her things to read every week.

In December, we returned to New Zealand to attend our son's graduation. When we did return to the village in January, we discovered this lady had already died. She had become ill and was taken to hospital by her family, but she said to them, 'Don't spend a whole lot of money on me. I'm ready to die.' So she was discharged from hospital, went home and died a few days later.

Was she saved? We have reason to believe so, and expect to meet her again in Heaven. This was a case of making a little extra effort in reaching someone who would or could not come to a meeting.

Being flexible and willing to use different approaches, even the unconventional, to reach the hard-to-reach people in every community is worth the effort and surely is what Jesus wants. As the parable of the soils confirms, the 'person of peace' in an unreached village may not be the first person you think of. Sometimes they are the seed on the stony soil, and after initial enthusiasm won't last.

It's sometimes said that funerals are good opportunities for the gospel. How about 'deathbed salvations?' Waew once had an opportunity to lead an elderly woman to Christ 20 minutes before she died. You can't cut it much finer than that. It occurred as we arrived to attend a church meeting at Pia Faan village. We were notified that a woman who lived across the road from the church sala (meeting place) was dying.

We went over to the house, where we found the woman lying on a mat surrounded by about 30 female relatives. While I waited at the edge of the room, Waew went right up and sat next to the elderly woman. She was conscious but weak. Waew simply explained that we are all sinners and God had provided a way for our sins to be paid for, which was through the Saviour Lord Jesus. She asked the woman if she would like to receive Jesus as her Saviour and that assurance of eternal life with Him. 'Oh yes, I would,' came the reply.

As relatives watched on in silence, Waew led this old lady in a prayer of repentance. She repeated Waew's words with a strong voice until about halfway through, when she continued quietly, her energy failing. At the end, Waew said the new believer continued to 'talk to God' by herself.

We left the scene to join the church meeting across the road. About 20 minutes later, during our worship time, a woman came from the house and simply said, 'She's gone.' Very quickly, we observed the men produce a waiting coffin while fireworks were set off. The Buddhists believe the spirit of a dead person will hang around for three days and the fireworks will scare the spirit away. But this lady was well gone before that, entering the presence of the Lord only 20 minutes after hearing His name.

We heard the following week that many in the family were awed by what they saw that day. They had never seen anything before like that at a deathbed vigil. Cultural customs were brushed aside to give a woman a last gasp opportunity of salvation.

Even the uninterested can be reached

How often do we give up on people too early? When we are talking about witnessing or sharing our faith in Jesus with someone (the dreaded 'E' word), the threshold for abandoning effort is fairly low for most Christians. We try turning the conversation to spiritual matters with someone, find a cold response, and we mentally note not to try that again with that person. But people can change.

As we walked around the villages in Isaan, we met many people who showed no interest in hearing about Jesus. And no, they didn't want one of our handout sheets to read.

At Pia Faan village, where we worked for three years, a man called Paw Samaan had no interest in talking to us. In the early days before a church was planted, we went house-to-house every week. He would turn his back when he saw us and walk away, so after a while we stopped bothering him. Obviously, he wasn't interested. But unbeknownst to us, his wife became a believer and came to the church meeting on Fridays. With all the people coming to the different church meetings, it was difficult to remember or know all the family relationships.

Finding the Keys

One day, we were wandering around Pia Faan before the church meeting and saw Paw Samaan's wife hurrying along the road towards us. She was hurrying home with a soymilk drink for her husband, who she explained was at home very sick and could not eat food. We said we'd come too and followed her into the house where we were previously unwelcome. There we saw Paw Samaan lying on a bed in the main room looking very ill. His body and face were very thin, mere skin stretched over his skull. We were told he hadn't been able to eat for days, and they were trying to give him fluids. The situation looked grave. We had seen people like this before and they were usually at death's door. Prayer was all we could offer and using the prayer of faith, we prayed for his healing, then had to move on to the church meeting.

A week later we dropped by at the house, not knowing what we would find. There in the doorway was Paw Samaan sitting on the floor and watching television. He enthusiastically welcomed us and acknowledged that after our prayer, he had recovered and was now healed and able to eat again.

Our arrival caused some excitement in the family. An adult son who had previously ignored us rushed inside to welcome us, and suddenly the knowledge of Jesus was welcome in that home. We left after gospel literature was gratefully accepted by Paw Samaan and his family. The uninterested had become interested in Jesus now they had a testimony.

We had a similar situation at another village. At two houses near where the church meets, we had left one of our own tracts every week for two years. At one house, we never saw anyone home, and at the other, a woman smiled but never came to any of the church meetings. It seemed like a waste of time and effort, but we persevered. Finally, one day, both women from these two houses came to the church meeting. We discovered their husbands had come to several church meetings a month earlier, and they gave permission for them to come as well. The seemingly uninterested had become interested after reading numerous tracts about Jesus. God was working in their hearts all along. But would this have happened if we had cut them off from that weekly gospel message a year or so earlier?

Keep on sowing that gospel seed

The more seed of the gospel we sow, the more likely we are to see the result of lives changed and Kingdom of God transformation in the communities we work in. We know from the Parable of the Soils that much of the seed the farmer sowed didn't end up producing a crop, but even in the poorest of seed beds we can expect some yield or crop.

When I studied Agronomy at university, we learnt about the gorse plant. This plant produces a hard seed that remains viable in the soil for up to 100 years before conditions are right for germination. For the gorse seed, it is often a fire that burns the vegetation to stimulate germination many decades later. The same can happen with the spiritual gospel seed we sow into people's lives.

One day, we began visiting a new village where we understood there were no Christians. On that first visit, we walked down the road leading into the village and greeted people who were out and about. Outside one house we asked an old man if any Christians lived in the village. He said there were some a long time ago, but they had died. Further on we stopped at a sala on the roadside, where a group of older women were seated relaxing. That day, Waew had brought her guitar, and we introduced ourselves and joined them.

Waew began playing her guitar, and we sang them an Isaan language gospel song, which several ladies clapped along to. After we had finished, a woman in her sixties got up and sang to us a Thai language version of 'Our God is so big,' even doing the hand and arm actions to this Sunday School children's song! We were stunned and asked her where she learnt the song. She replied that about 50 years earlier, some missionaries used to visit the village on Sunday and collect children in a truck to take them to a Sunday School at a church in the city. This woman was one of the children that went to the programme. She said the missionaries stopped coming to the village a long time ago, but a few people had become believers, though they had now died. Amongst the young, the seeds of the gospel had remained in the soil.

Several older ladies who had been to the Sunday School became the founding members of the church we later were able to plant in the village of Nong Ping. It was wonderful that we were able to harvest the seed sown by earlier missionaries and see a maturing faith in these women 50 years after they had first heard the name of Jesus and of the 'God who was so big.' It reminded us that in many ways, we are standing on the shoulders of those servants who have gone before and that God's Word will not return void but will accomplish what He intends.

Another thing that we always noticed about Nong Ping was it was, in many ways, one of the easiest villages in which to plant a church. The fruit fell into our hands, and there was little of the spiritual and social opposition we experienced in some villages. In fact, even the village leader (the Phuyaibaan) would drop in and join church meetings and was very friendly. Though he was a Buddhist, his grandfather had been one of these early Christians. The whole spiritual atmosphere was different. We just knew someone had been praying for this village.

Top: Bible reading at a village church meeting.
Bottom: Kingdom growth; every one a new believer.

Finding the Keys

Top: A church meeting at a sala.
Bottom: Spiritual food.

*Top: Another sala location for a church meeting.
Bottom: Bible reading at every meeting.*

Top: Communion at a village church.
Bottom: Reaching the next generation.

CHAPTER 7

Keys in the Cultural Traditions that Can Open the Door to the Gospel

The 'Phra See Ahn prophecy' and its significance to Northeast Thailand Buddhists

Has God, who prepared the gospel for all peoples, also prepared all peoples for the gospel? Missionary, Don Richardson, explores this question in his book *Eternity in their Hearts*. In it, he shows that in stories and oral traditions from many different cultures, people had a concept of a supreme God and these stories and traditions have often prepared them to receive the gospel. This is the idea of 'redemptive analogies' used by God to draw all people to Himself.

It was some time after we had been in Northeast Thailand that we began to hear references to 'Phra See Ahn,' usually from older village people. In oral traditions in the Northeast, there is a prophecy about a messiah-like figure who comes after the Buddha and in effect, perfects his work or achieves things the Buddha could not. When we talked to village people, the older ones had memories of being told about Phra See Ahn by village monks. As the village people described this figure, it was always a coming figure who would perfect all things. Often this name cropped up when we were sharing the gospel stories about Jesus. People were struck by how Jesus seemed to fit perceptions of what Phra See Ahn would do and who he was.

Finding the Keys

We made inquiries and discovered other missionaries had encountered the Phra See Ahn prophecy over the years, but most hadn't investigated it fully. One who had was Paul DeNeui, an early advocate of a contextualised approach to reaching Buddhists in Northeast Thailand.

The thought occurred to us that this prophecy may pre-date Buddhism and be one of those 'eternity in their hearts' stories that occur in various cultural traditions. Some years ago, we had read the books by Don Richardson that showed there were keys God seems to have left to unlock cultures to the knowledge of God. Could it be that the Phra See Ahn prophecy was one of these ancient stories dispersed with the tribes as they migrated across the globe?

What we had heard was that Phra See Ahn would come after the Buddha and achieve for ordinary people what the Buddha could not. In some versions, the prophecy was an oral tradition that the Buddha told to his disciples, but the original story may be older than Buddhism and simply modified by Buddhist monks later.

Some of the striking aspects of the prophecy of Phra See Ahn was that when he came, he would not be recognised and accepted by the people. His coming would mean an equality between all people, which contrasts with the spiritual hierarchy between Buddhist monks and laity. 'The outcasts and lepers will become the best' seems to echo some of Jesus' sayings and parables such as 'the first shall be last.'

The following is the transcript of an interview done in the Isaan language by Paul DeNeui (P) with Mr Khampan Sudcha (K), a 38-year-old Thai evangelist working for the Lower Isaan Foundation for Enablement (LIFE) in Roi Et, Northeast Thailand. The conversation was taped on January 2, 2004, and later translated into English by Paul DeNeui.

'Many people waiting for Phra See Ahn are actually waiting for Jesus.'

P: Let me ask you about the Buddhist prophecy of Phra See Ahn. I understand it speaks of one who was to come. Who is Phra See Ahn, and what is this prophecy all about?

K: Understand that this legend is primarily significant to those [Northeastern Thai] who are now at least 60 years old or older. For young people today, it is not meaningful anymore; however, the story of Phra See Ahn is still told in some places. I myself heard it from my elders and from the 'maw lom' singing when I was growing up.

P: Do you believe that this prophecy about Phra See Ahn is referring to Jesus?

K: Yes. It is about Jesus.

P: Did this prophecy come before the Buddhist era?

K: No, it started in the Buddhist era since some parts of it still remain to be fulfilled. [In our Northeastern Thai culture] there is the [written] Buddhist teaching and there is the oral teaching. The oral teachings are the legends that have been passed down from generation to generation; some of these are prophecies that have to do with Buddhism. The legend of the Phra See Ahn is from our oral teaching.

P: Is there anything in the oral tradition that alludes to those who would believe first?

K: Yes. Mostly, it has been young people who have responded to the message of Jesus before their parents. This is also true in the Yoreh group [a cult]. They say that Phra See Ahn has come. I have talked to several of their members who say that Phra See Ahn is coming to relieve the world and that those who came after Buddha are part of him. But when I ask them to translate what they are saying, they are unable to do so.

P: After listening to your explanation of Phra See Ahn, have there been some who have made a decision of faith and followed Christ?

K: Yes. There are several who have believed because of explaining it. Father Lee [in Roi Et] was one. Many of the older generation who have become God's children in Roi Et have believed because of having this prophecy explained to them. I can say that hundreds of these people are children of God [Christians]. They have come to know God because of the prophecy of Phra See Ahn, the one they were anticipating.

P: Are you saying that this anticipation has prepared them to receive God?

K: Yes. Many people waiting for Phra See Ahn are actually waiting for Jesus.

P: What can you tell me about the person of Phra See Ahn from the prophecy?

K: Can you explain the meaning of Phra See Ahn or [as his name is fully said] Phra See Arriyah Meht Tri Yoh? Do you know what this name means?

P: No. Tell me about it.

K: You have to translate back to the root words of Phra See Arriyah Meht Tri Yoh. Start with the second word, 'see.' This word comes from the Sanskrit root 'seeri,' which means 'excellent' or 'full of glory.' But the Bible says that all people have sinned and have fallen short of God's glory (Romans 3:23). However, when Jesus came, he was born a human just like us but full of God's glory (John 1:13-14).

Jesus was born with 'seeri,' God's glory. The word 'glory' is the same [Thai] root word found in the [Thai] term for 'excellent.' We don't try to force our own meaning on these words, but we are trying to understand what the heart meaning is of the words in the scripture and the words that people are using. In Buddhism, this word is translated this same way.

So put this together with the first pronoun, 'Phra' [the honorific for a Holy One], and you have 'Phra See,' the most glorious Holy One. A Holy One does not have sin. Jesus did not have a wife, nor did he father any children; therefore, in the Thai way of thinking he did not have sin. But if an ordinary person fathers children, he is considered less than perfect and therefore has sin.

The next term, 'arriyah,' means 'big' in the sense of 'all-powerful.' For example, when we say the Thai word, 'arriyaprathet,' this means a large, powerful country. Or the word 'arriyahtham,' which means a 'great, powerful teaching.' Another word is 'arriyasatsee,' which means 'the Four Noble Truths of Buddhism.' But the term 'Phra See Arriyah' means the all-powerful, glorious Holy One. And who could be greater or more powerful than the one who created the heavens and the earth? All other religious leaders were born after the creation of the world, but Jesus was the Word who existed with the Father and was the Father before the creation of the world.

People who hear this get excited. They start to see what they have been waiting for in the Phra See Arriyah Meht Tri. If the terms are explained word by word, they can understand.

The next word, 'meht,' comes from the word 'meddha.' This means merciful and kind – an action towards other people. Therefore, when we put these words together, Phra See Arriyah Meht means the all-powerful, glorious Holy One who acts in mercy. We say [another part of the Phra See Ahn prophecy]:

'Kee tood ko tang jah dai kert ben dee.'
[The outcasts and lepers will become the best.]

When he comes, all will be without sin. This means that, for example, even an old grandmother out in her field will be able to go to heaven because someone can read the Bible to her, and she can understand it herself and go to heaven. Those who were born in the poorest and lowest levels of society will be reborn in sinless excellence. They will find God before others. I usually give the example of the poor villagers. Who in the village finds God first? It is the poorest of the poor when they experience the mercy and kindness of God in their lives. When they understand the Bible teaching that God loved them so much that he was even willing to die for them, they see that there is only one willing to do that. This is Jesus, the merciful and kind one who they were waiting to come.

I tell people that if they don't believe me to go ahead and study it for themselves and see if the root meaning of this name is what I am explaining or not. Buddha is not the merciful one because if any person is not born with all 32 parts, then that person cannot become a monk. Also, in order to be a Buddhist monk, a person must be born male.

The word 'tri' means three. This is the same as the Thai flag that has three colours and is known as the tritrong [three-coloured flag]. For Isaan people, the 'three' part of this title refers to heaven, earth, and hell. The Great One has a love that reaches into all three places. We understand that heaven is the place of God. The earth is the place God created. Hell is the dwelling place of Satan and his demons. God is greater than all three of these places; he takes care of all three levels. Buddha is not able to do this. Opening to the beginning of the Bible, people can read about the God who created the earth and is the owner of the heavens and the earth. This is the meaning of the One in Three, all-powerful, glorious Holy One who acts in mercy. Old people hear this and have to admit that it is the truth.

The final word is 'yoh,' from 'yowah.' This comes from the word that means wind. This points to the Holy Spirit, who is described as the wind. He is not referred to in physical terms as a person, but he can be experienced as wind or as fire. People can see what he does. Thai people have another proverb that says when Phra See Ahn comes: 'Man jah raahb bai ben muan nah kong fai' [All will be equal just as fire evens everything in its path].

I can translate all of this. This means that even if you are a wealthy millionaire living on the fifth floor of a tall building and you drive a Mercedes-Benz, or you are simply a poor farmer riding on the buffalo's back, one day all will be made equal because all who have Jesus will be equally saved. The way I translate it fits perfectly with the proverb. This is an explanation that really speaks to the heart of the poor! God says, 'It is me! Come on in!' People listen carefully to all of this. When I speak with elderly people, they especially become very interested.

All of this has to do with faith. People look for and wait for the one who is to come all their life and never find him if they don't understand the meaning. *All these older traditions have an origin and a purpose. Explaining the meaning is what I do when speaking with older people.*

P: Should missionaries use this method with older Thai people?

K: I think using this with older people brings results because they have a background in Buddhism.

P: Would this be true of Buddhists from all parts of Thailand?

K: Yes. All older Thai people are familiar with this. They are still waiting for Phra See Ahn to arrive.

P: What about the younger generation? What do they know about Phra See Ahn?

K: The way to present the gospel to the younger generation is not simply to talk at them. We have to present the gospel in ways that young people can connect with personally. Those young people who have found God can now share what God has done for them in their lives. You can see results in their lives; they have gone very far already – as far as the sun! Their lives have changed radically through their experience of God. This experience with God is what convinces young people today that God is real. Young people are experiencing things all the time now, especially through the media. They see things on television, they see the President [of the United States], and they see many, many things that are relevant to their world today.

If we talk about heaven or hell to young people, it has no relevance to them because to them, these things [if they exist at all for them] are far off in the distance. I share about things that are related to today, the events that hit us in our daily lives. This is the method I use in sharing with young people because these things are easy to talk about. This doesn't make young people sleepy [or turn them off].

P: So you're saying you don't teach about Phra See Ahn.

K: No. This is not necessary. They don't know anything about it. There are songs that I lead them in singing and this builds interest. There are a number of popular tunes I frequently use as a way to build interest with young people.

P: Do you think this explanation of Phra See Ahn should be translated for other missionaries to understand?

K: That is up to you if you want to do it. I once bought a book about Phra See Ahn. It explained some of the meanings that I have described but not in much detail. It said that when Phra See Ahn really comes, he would be like Buddha. It said he would be born in a heavenly place and would live with all the thousands of female angelic beings. He would have a wife and would not be born into this world. The author of this book was not teaching the complete story.

If we look at this as followers of Jesus, we can see the meanings in these Thai prophecies. There are three things in these prophecies and three in our beliefs. We have the Father, the Son, and the Holy Spirit. Buddhists have the Buddha, the Dhamma, and the Sangha. All religions have a basis of three that do not disagree with each other.

If I were to suggest studying Buddhism in order to compare how it conflicts with Christianity, then you should get ready to run [i.e., people will respond violently]. This is because we need to respect Buddhism; it was here before we were. People have become deeply attached to their cultural beliefs. What Buddha taught was true. I ask people, 'Do you know what Buddha taught?' [Another quote from the prophecy]:

'Haak wah than mah tung leaw khon buah nai.'
[When he comes people will not accept him.]

Buddha taught that when the One came, people would not accept him and would not welcome him. If Jesus did not want people to follow him, why did he come to die for everyone? I ask the person listening to me – is this true? Grandpa is listening to me, and he says, 'It's true!'

I ask him, 'Did Jesus come and tell you off? Has he done something to wrong you? If not, why do people hate him?'

'Houay!' he says. 'I haven't got the faintest idea. All I know is that when I hear the name "Jesus," I get furious.'

So, I say to Grandpa, 'Do you see that what the Buddha said is true?'

He says, 'Yes, I see that now.'

When the Buddha said that the one to come would be rejected, he spoke the truth. People who are listening are starting to pay serious attention at this point.

What else did Buddha teach? He taught that those who go to heaven are like the horns of a cow, but those who go to hell are like the hairs on the hide.

I ask Grandpa, 'Which are more on the cow – the horns or the hairs? Most people say the horns are fewer. So, I ask, 'Grandpa, in your village, how many people are following Jesus?'

He says, 'Not very many.'

I summarise by sharing that even Buddha himself taught that only a few would follow the one to come. I ask him, 'Did Buddha lie to us?'

'No,' he will say. 'Buddha did not lie.'

So I ask him, 'If you don't believe yet, why don't you consider what you are saying?'

We are trying to encourage the use of the beliefs that people already have so that they can see that what they believe in is really the truth. I tried to write this up once but writing it out and speaking it in dialogue with people is very different. I must say that any specific method is not going to work in every situation. It is only a principle or a foundation from which to build. Actually putting these ideas into practice is a completely different story. In reality, all of this is the work of the Holy Spirit, who is working in the heart of the person with whom we are speaking.

P: Thank you for sharing this with me.

Our use of the Phra See Ahn story

It seemed to us a key was available in this Isaan story, and we began to make references to the Phra See Ahn tradition in our work in the villages. The result among the older village people (over 60 years old) was that it was an effective bridge to the cultural thinking and beliefs. It was a way of saying, 'Look, even your own traditions speak of a coming Saviour who will accomplish things the Buddha could not.' Used in this context, it was similar to Paul's use of the sayings of Greek philosophers and poets in Acts 17:28-29. These sayings contain some truth, although imperfect, but it does open the door for the truth as revealed in the Word. As Mr Khampan mentions, this story is not well known among the younger generation, so would really only be useful in reaching the elderly generation, but they are the majority living in villages, so we still see a place for using this story. Perhaps the fact that the monks don't talk much about Phra See Ahn these days is because they have become aware of the opening the story has for introducing Jesus.

CHAPTER 8

The Key of Prayer

So far, we have talked about the need in Thailand for the good news of Jesus Christ and some of the keys we uncovered during our time there. There is one key that links everything together, and that is the 'Key of Prayer.'

Nothing much will change in Thailand if no one speaks the gospel to people, and nothing much will change without the prayers of the saints, be they local Christians or offshore intercessors. Prayer really is a vital key in breaking up the 'hard ground' for the seed of the gospel to be sowed into. Mission effort that is not soaked in prayer will often see minimal fruit result. Mission activity in tandem with prayer, particularly the prayer of supporters who meet specifically to pray for Thailand, or a particular ministry, is vital.

For foreign workers in Thailand, this covering of prayer from a regular prayer group is essential. Missions' prayer meetings focused on workers in the field and ministry objectives are like air force support to the front-line soldiers, where the praying partners know the situation the worker faces, the ministry focus, goals and problems. Prayer can move events supernaturally to turn a situation around or make a way where there seems to be none.

When we served in Thailand, we were blessed by having a team of supporters at home who prayed for us both individually and at a monthly prayer meeting for Northeast Thailand. A Christian worker who goes to Thailand without this sort of committed regular prayer cover and support is at a much higher risk of spiritual attack. When people are thinking about going to Thailand in ministry, it's not just about finances and who will provide money. Equally important is who will pray for you and your work? In fact, if no one makes a commitment to pray for you, it would be better not to go.

The Bible shows us God consistently does his work in partnership with willing servants and always with people who will pray. God wants nations to follow him and heed His Word. In Matthew 25:32, we read of whole nations being judged and separated from Him. Nations who are faithful to God separated from nations that are unfaithful. God's heart is for reaching the nations like Thailand, nations that have not traditionally followed Him. We see this in the Book of Jonah. There we find God's extraordinary concern for the heathen nation of Assyria and its major city, Ninevah, a powerful and proud city of a cruel nation that God sent one man to preach repentance to. The amazing part of the story of Jonah (outside of the whale incident) was despite his reluctance to help (he was a reluctant servant), God still moved in hearts, and people repented and were saved from God's judgement.

But others of God's servants in the Bible had purer motives. These servants had a zeal and compassion for the lost and rebellious. And it is a zeal and compassion in people who pray that is needed to see these hard-to-reach nations reached. The people who take up this cause are what we call intercessors, and Moses was a good example. His intercession was a natural development of his intimacy with God. In Exodus 33:11, we read, 'The Lord would speak to Moses face to face, as a man speaks to his friend.' From that level of relationship, Moses had the boldness to ask questions and intercede for others. Moses identified himself with his people and 'stepped into the gap' frequently when the people became rebellious.

In Romans chapter 9, the Apostle Paul reveals his own zeal and compassion for his Jewish countrymen and women. 'I have great sorrow and unceasing anguish in my heart' (Romans 9:2).

Paul would rather God took his life if it meant his people would repent.

The Intercessor

I urge, then, first of all, that requests, prayers, intercession and thanksgiving be made for everyone. (1 Timothy 2:1)

Every Christian is called to be a patriot in the true sense, having a heart for their own nation.

To some, God gives the heart for a foreign nation. In that place of interceding, we then recognise the national sin of that nation in whatever area of rebellion against God's law. We need to learn to listen to God and be in tune to Him. In a way, we act as being responsible for that nation as an intercessor. It's an important role, and one few others are taking on, but it's a vitally important one. How many today are praying for Thailand and the Isaan region?

Sometimes God is looking around for even for one person to take on the intercessor role, but can he find someone? In Isaiah 59:16, we read, 'He saw there was no one, he was appalled that there was no one to intercede.' And in Jeremiah 33:3, we see God's eagerness to partner with us as we pray: 'Call to me and I will answer you and tell you great and unsearchable things for you to know.'

In intercession, the praying person is 'standing between' God and the object of the prayer, i.e. people, a nation, or a situation. The intercessor does four things:

1) Prays to hold off God's judgement.

2) Petitions God specifically on behalf of others.
3) Stands between Satan and the object of prayer.
4) Specifically resists Satan and his influence.

A good Biblical example is in Acts 12:5 after King Herod had arrested Peter: 'So Peter was kept in prison, but the church was *earnestly praying to God for him.*' The result was a miraculous escape aided by an angel.

We might wonder why God even requires an intercessor, but it's related to the way God has given authority on earth to people. God acts as we specifically pray. But many prayers prayed are not specific enough. 'Oh God, save people' is too vague. To the degree and specificness with which we pray, God will move in the lives of people. We need to pray detailing the who, what, when, why and where of the need.

Spiritual warfare

A key aspect of our prayer for Thailand is what is referred to as spiritual warfare. This is prayer war against the evil spirit powers that Paul highlights in Ephesians 6:12: 'For our struggle is not against flesh and blood but against the rulers, against the authorities against the powers of this dark world and against the spiritual forces of evil in the heavenly realms.' Paul then advises the Christian to put on the spiritual armour God has provided to us.

In praying for Thailand and breakthrough for the gospel, we are struggling in prayer not against people (flesh and blood) but against invisible evil forces of Satan who conspire to keep the nation in darkness. The church and individual intercessors must be on the offensive, taking the battle to the enemy, claiming territory, binding and loosing, and assailing strongholds so the captives are set free. The church must be on the offensive, as how can the Gates of Hell not prevail if they are not attacked?

The Christian's role is to take the battle to the 'enemy' (Satan and his forces), opposing his false ideas whenever found with the goal of seeing people released into freedom that comes in Christ. Equally, being a spiritual battle, the weapons used are spiritual not physical: 'We do not fight with weapons of the world' (2 Corinthians 10:4). 'We demolish arguments and every pretension that sets itself up against the knowledge of God, and we take captive every thought and make it obedient to Christ' (2 Corinthians 10:5).

The key point to note here is the Christian deals vigorously with the forces of Satan but gently with the people of the world.

God has provided every believer a spiritual armour and we must know how to use it (see Ephesians 6:10-20). The 'Armour of God' is an important study in itself. We won't cover that in detail here, but it is vital that any worker in Thailand, or intercessor, has experience in the use of this spiritual resource which God has provided. Special mention in the context of intercession should be made of the 'Sword of the Spirit,' this being the only offensive/attacking part of the Armour of God. Paul specifically tells us the Sword of the Spirit is the Word of God (verse 17). Notice that Satan will only flee from the Word of God. The Sword of the Spirit is living and sharper than any two-edged (natural) sword. The Word of God in this context is not just scripture, but all 'words that come from God' by His Spirit. The Greek word Paul uses in verse 17 for 'word' is 'rhema', signifying the spoken word, which is significant from a prayer and intercession perspective.

Lessons from the fig tree

In Mark 11:12-24, we read of the curious incident of the fig tree that wilted after Jesus cursed it. Jesus used this incident and the surprise of his disciples to teach them about faith in God and what he can do in response to our prayers. But it requires us operating in the 'faith of God' (1 Corinthians 12:9).

> *'Have faith in God,' Jesus answered. 'Truly I tell you, if anyone says to this mountain, 'Go throw yourself into the sea' and does not doubt in his heart, but believes that what he says will happen, it will be done for him. Therefore, I tell you, whatever you ask for in prayer, believe that you have received it, and it will be yours.' (Mark 11:22-24)*

Jesus was giving an illustration of a prayer for an 'impossible' situation. He had just spoken to a tree, and it had died. In the natural scheme of things, mountains don't fly off to bathe in the sea. The situation seems almost absurd, but this is a faith-stretching problem Jesus is highlighting. The entrenched religion of Buddhism in Thailand is like a mountain. It is seemingly unmovable. But for the believer with the faith of God, who is operating in that spiritual gift, miracles can happen. Breakthroughs can occur.

A key here is taking authority over the problem (the mountain) and causing it to be removed. A second key is to pray with faith, believing we will receive what we ask for. Notice in verse 14 Jesus decreed something to happen: 'No one will ever eat fruit from you again.' This was the way he released his faith; he spoke out his thoughts. We can also, in faith, decree life-giving things. We can, in faith, decree certain things to happen that line up with the will of God. We can decree victory over certain situations (Job 22:28). We can decree healing to occur (Matthew 18:18).

After cursing the fig tree, Jesus went on his way to Jerusalem. He had no reason to stay as he knew the result would come. Faith always sees the thing as done, even if the result is not instantly visible.

The withering of the fig tree began from the roots: 'they saw the fig tree withered from the roots' (verse 20). We can decree something to occur in faith, such as healing or salvation to come to people of a village, and in doing so, we are exercising faith. And when we pray, we need to see those roots dealt with first. The roots speak of the source of nourishment and life for the structure above. As roots feed the leafy canopy above a tree, in a spiritual sense, false religions and ideologies are fed by a life force from Satan. If that is cut off, the top growth will wither, so this is part of the way we wage spiritual warfare. We are praying and interceding using various means; asking in prayer, decreeing, and using at times a word of command ('go throw yourself in the sea'). All these need to be operated in faith.

Now faith is a developing thing. It's like a muscle in our body. The more it is used, the stronger it will become. Faith develops by hearing the Word of God. This is the food for our faith. Faith also develops by experience, by our acting on our faith and exercising our faith. If our faith is only developed a small amount, we will only be able to take on small problems. Regarding faith, there is also a biblical principle of receiving what you have faith for (Matthew 9:29), but sometimes God can work beyond what we have faith for (Ephesians 3:20). These are times when God goes beyond our faith and an unexpected miracle occurs. The important thing is to pray in faith. God will act according to the power of God working within us.

Faith of the persistent

During a quiet visit to Tyre, Jesus and the disciples get an uninvited visit from a Syrophoenician (Greek) woman (see Mark 7:21

and Matthew 15:21-28). Surprisingly, Jesus ignored the woman for a time, but she was not put off and persevered in her request. God sometimes doesn't answer our prayers straight away, but he has heard them.

When it seems like we are getting no answer, keep asking! Don't give up. The woman was not put off by the frosty reception. Jesus was teaching her (and us) that we need to press into him and not give up. She got her request and was commended as having 'great faith.'

In Luke 11:5-10, when Jesus was teaching about prayer, he tells a parable about a man visiting his friend at night, asking for bread to put before guests at his house. The man initially refuses, but after the friend shows no sign of leaving without the bread, gets up and gives him what he wants.

In both examples, people push on beyond the socially polite boundary to receive what they need. God wants his people to have the same shameless abandon to ask and keep asking until the request is granted.

The same idea comes through with the Parable of the Unjust Judge in Luke 18. The woman's persistence in her request caused the judge, who was unfair, to give her what she wanted to get rid of her. God is not unjust, but Jesus said God would answer to the degree we pray. This persistency and the fervency will release God's hands. The more we intercede, the more we can be effective in releasing God to act.

Some intercession prayer suggestions

1) *2 Corinthians 4:4*

The god of this age has blinded the minds of the unbelievers, so that they cannot see the light of the gospel that displays the glory of Christ, who is the image of God.

Reflection: We used this scripture on our first ministry advertising brochures back in 2006, as even back then we saw it as a scripture that described Thailand. The scripture states well the reason so few Thai people have received the Good News of the gospel even after 150 years of missionary activity. There is a spiritual reason for the blockage, and that spiritual blindness must be dealt with in each individual Buddhist before they will be able to 'see' the truth.

Prayer: This inspires targeted prayer for opening of eyes by God, but also use of the authority already given to believers to bind the works of Satan and cast down ideas that have set themselves up in opposition to the knowledge of God.

Personalising it: As witnesses and intercessors, our role is to both co-operate with the Holy Spirit and seek His intervention in others' lives and also to use the authority given to us in engaging in spiritual warfare for the lost. We must be active, not passive, witnesses.

2) *Ephesians 2:8-9*

For it is by grace you have been saved, through faith – and this not from yourselves, it is the gift of God – not by works, so no one can boast.

Reflection: This scripture is a full-on, frontal challenge to the Buddhist mind. Buddhism is in reality a 'self-help' religion. A person saves themselves by their own efforts to do good deeds, earning positive karma points to offset the bad karma points sin incurs. But in this scripture, Paul points out that the only way we are saved is by 'grace, through faith' in what the Saviour Jesus has already done. Further efforts of 'making merit' is pointless and futile, as 2,000 years ago the price was paid. We cannot earn our own salvation by works (trying to be good), which is the very thing Buddhists attempt to do. As Jesus said on the cross, 'It is finished!'

Prayer: We need to pray that the Buddhist people we are trying to reach with the gospel will gain revelation that their merit-making efforts are futile and will not pay for their sins. Pray also that conviction would come as to their need for the Saviour, Jesus Christ, to rescue them from this doctrine of karma and self-effort.

Personalising it: All of us have fallen short of the glory of God and are in need of God's grace. Therefore, we express our gratefulness that the victory won on the cross carries forward for all time and is received as a gift and is not earned.

Other prayer focus areas

1) The Government of Thailand. Thailand has had a succession of democratically elected governments followed by military coups. The current government evolved out of a military coup. There is a long history of politicians serving themselves and enriching themselves rather than serving the country.

2) The Thai Church. Some of the issues relating to the church and its activity, or lack thereof, have been identified in this book and is another area where prayer is needed.

3) Workers for the Harvest Field. The need is as great as ever,

both for local workers, supported by local churches, and for foreign missionaries to continue preaching the gospel to those yet to hear.

4) Pray for the 'harder-to-reach fruit.'

5) Pray about starting a prayer meeting focused on Thailand and particularly the Isaan people of the Northeast region.

CHAPTER 9

The Call of God to Missions

Then I heard the voice of the Lord saying, 'Whom shall I send? And who will go for us?'
And I said, 'Here am I. Send me!' (Isaiah 6:8)

Sometimes God singles out people for service, such as the call of Jeremiah the prophet and the Apostle Paul. But most people who hear the call hear it while walking in relationship with Him. And it's more a case of God revealing a need.

Look at the relaxed and friendly way Jesus called his 12 disciples, with a smile, a hand on the shoulder, and a look into their eyes as he said, 'Follow me!' If we allow the Holy Spirit to bring us into the presence of God, we also will hear and respond to his call.

Now we can sometimes think God will surely call us to things that interest us, or we have ability in. Not necessarily. Some might experience that, others not. Paul wrote that the Lord told him, 'For my power is made perfect in weakness.' It's not necessarily a case of what I would like to do for God. People with the gift of service can fall into that trap, like Martha, and miss God's best.

Paul writes about his call in Galatians 1:12: 'I did not receive it from any man, nor was I taught it, rather I received it by revelation from Jesus Christ.' Then in verse 15: 'But when God... was pleased to reveal his son in me so that I might preach him among the Gentiles... I did not consult any man.'

And when we do serve Him, it should be the outflow of devoted love for God. God leads us into a relationship with himself whereby I understand his call, then I do things for him out of sheer love for him.

A little of our story

In 1989, I (Peter) had been on several short-term mission trips to Indonesia, but while I felt a stirring about missions, I didn't recognise a call at that stage.

There was a mid-week meeting at a church in Whakatane where the speaker was Dr Paul Kaufman, the founder of the mission organisation, Asian Outreach. I went along to listen to him speak. He was a man in his eighties, a missionary giant, born in China in 1908 to missionary parents, a fluent Mandarin speaker, imprisoned by the Japanese during World War Two. At the end of the meeting, he asked people to come forward if they were available to God for overseas mission service, and he would pray. In a way, he was suggesting we invite God to *'help himself to our lives.'* I went forward that day with a dozen others and felt something stir in my heart. God noticed.

1) *A Call from God is between a person and God*
God calls people personally. There are some things all Christians are expected to do. Personal witnessing of their faith is one. That's not a specific Call of God. That is a general expectation of all believers. But God speaks personally to the people he calls, such as Noah, Moses, and Abraham. Notice that God didn't send someone to tell them they were called. Nowhere in the Bible did other people show someone what their calling was.

However, God will often use other experienced Christians to

confirm our call. This confirmation is to give us assurance we have heard correctly, and that it wasn't just 'that pizza we ate.'

In John 20:21, on the night after his resurrection, Jesus commissions his disciples, saying, 'As the Father has sent me, I am sending you.' A missionary is someone sent by Jesus Christ as He was sent by God the Father. And the key factor here is not so much the need or the work we do but obedience to the will of God. The Call of God is, by definition, a supernatural encounter with God. It's not something we can analyse and explain in technical detail. It's like trying to explain love. In fact, if we can fully explain our call, it probably isn't a genuine call from God.

This realisation that God's call is upon you may come suddenly and dramatically (think Paul) or in a gradual dawning. But whatever way it comes, there is this supernatural undercurrent, something you cannot put satisfactorily into words. *'You know because you know.'* There is a sudden consciousness of this call, and it's taken hold of your life.

2) *God, not the individual Christian, must be the first mover*

The Call of God does not come from our pastor or our parents or group leader. It is God who calls people into roles of service in the church, or it should be. Christian leaders will sometimes think of where they need help and then appoint people rather than letting God call them to that role. People in ministry should be there because they heard a call from God, not because they didn't have better employment options.

In Thailand, we met Christians on staff with a youth mission organisation. If you asked them about their ministry calling, many of them were unsure how to answer. They were doing what their leader had asked them to do rather than hearing a call from God. They didn't say, 'My calling is Youth Ministry, or Evangelism, or Mercy Ministry' or whatever. They didn't know.

Waew and I met in Thailand in 1991 while I was there working on a Dairy Farming development project. It wasn't missionary work, but God had a reason for me to be there. I didn't know that at the time, but it was firstly to be made aware of the need for the gospel in rural Thailand, and secondly to meet my future wife and helpmate in ministry. When you seek God's will for your life, He really does 'order your steps.' We got married about six months after meeting, and this year will be 30 years of marriage.

We returned to New Zealand in 1993, lived initially in Morrinsville, then in 1994 moved to Hamilton when I (Peter) got a job with the National Bank as a Rural Manager. We started attending a church, now known as Activate Church. It was already a large church but not greatly involved in overseas missions at the time. Within a couple of years, God brought in other new members who were former missionaries and people who one of the pastors would describe as 'Missions Passionates,' and the whole global missions focus took off from the mid-1990s. Waves of people went out as missionaries.

It seemed a constant stream of people from the church were presenting themselves as having the Call to Missions. And that will happen whenever church leadership encourages a focus on overseas missions. Churches that do not send or support overseas missionaries tend to have leadership that is not interested.

3) *The Call is always a matter of heart-searching and evaluation*
The thing about the call is it touches you very deeply. The more seriously you view your call and the more prayer and commitment you put into it, the clearer it becomes. When we realise God has a calling for each of us, we will start praying, fasting and reading the Word. We feel compelled.

When a person discovers his/her calling, they have a feeling of 'Eureka, I've found it! This is it! The will of God for my life!' And when a person discovers their calling, they will *dream about the ministry*, like a man in love dreams about his fiancé. It's always on your mind. You think about ways to accomplish that ministry or enter that ministry. And finally, the person with a call will *talk about it*... always! They will always want to talk about it, talk about the country they want to work in and the unreached people group that live there, and you will find them at missions' prayer meetings.

It is important, however, to *evaluate our motivation* at this stage. You see, our motivation should be love and wanting to obey God rather than find work to do. Do we love God and people? Our motivation should not be to serve out of fear of God, nor should it be to gain rewards from God. If it is, we have a wrong concept and wrong relationship with the Father.

4) *The specific nature of my call will come in time from God*
At the church at Antioch (Acts 13), the Holy Spirit spoke in prophecy: 'Set apart Paul and Barnabas for the work I have called them.' The revelation came 'while they were worshipping and fasting.' Possibly Paul and Barnabas were already thinking about this work, but it was the Holy Spirit who interrupted and confirmed the call.

Notice the Spirit didn't map out a strategic plan or vision statement for this new mission to Asia Minor. The Holy Spirit simply said, 'they have work to do'. The details and methodology came later.

Don't worry initially about the nature of your call. The details and specifics come later. The fuzziness goes in time, and focus becomes sharper. Another example is when Timothy walked with God, then the Holy Spirit identified him as an evangelist, and then Paul commissioned him.

When we left New Zealand in May 2006, all we could say was we were called to reach rural people in Northeast Thailand and plant churches. At that stage, we had no clear idea how that might happen.

Early on in your call, it's normal to be a bit vague as to details. Someone will say, 'How will you support yourself? How will you cover your costs?' You have no clear answer. All you can say is, 'I don't know, but I do know I am called.

These calls often develop slowly. Some people can trace their call back to childhood, perhaps Sunday school or even a dream. For others, you know immediately it is the Call of God. Perhaps some people reading this book will feel a stirring in their hearts as they are reading.

God told Paul in Acts 9 that he would show him what he wanted him to do. Paul knew he was called, but he didn't know right away what the ministry would look like. And God can and does use both our natural and spiritual giftings in our ministry.

When Waew and I arrived in Northeast Thailand in May 2006, we had some rough ideas how a ministry might begin, but nothing clear as to a strategy. It began for us unexpectedly when God broke through during an unplanned visit to a village. Waew took the initiative on a visit to a village with younger people from the ministry we were working with. They shared the gospel and prayed for healing for the sick. When they left, several villagers had received Christ and a woman's leg was instantly healed.

I asked our team leader who was going to follow up and disciple these new believers and got a vague, non-committal answer. Waew and I decided we would go, and that was the beginning of a church planted after only six months in Thailand. Something other missionaries said was impossible. The woman with the healed leg opened her home for church meetings.

5) The Call of God is inescapable and progressive

You can't run from it. Well, you can try, but that didn't work out too well for Jonah. If you have the Call of God on your life it follows you wherever you go.

Jeremiah was called as a child. Whatever your call, it will stay with you all your life.

If you are called to preach, it will stay with you.

Paul, writing in 1 Corinthians 9:16, says, 'Yet when I preach I cannot boast, for I am compelled to preach, woe to me if I do not preach the gospel.' Paul was eager to preach Christ, you can see the passion in his calling. People with a calling have a *passion* and enthusiasm that comes from God. It's Holy Spirit inspired. God will find a work for our calling, no matter what the calling is.

The call is also *progressive*. It develops over time and generally with an upward progression. When God reveals himself to men and women, it is in stages. And the idea there is that we don't receive so much that we can't take it in and absorb it. God always gives us what we can receive at the time.

From the time we first alerted the church missions team that God was calling us back to Thailand until the time we left for Thailand, a period of a year and a half passed. We were prayed for at a church service. The pastors and elders laid hands upon us and commissioned us as missionaries, literally 'sent ones.'

At that last meeting, a man came up to us and gave us a piece of paper with a prophetic word: 'As you have prepared here in New Zealand, God has prepared a place for you. You will see much harvest, and quickly,' and Isaiah 41:9-10: 'So do not fear, for I am with you, do not be dismayed, for I am your God, I will strengthen you and help you, I will uphold you with my righteous right hand.'

Ten days later, we were at our first team meeting with a ministry in Northeast Thailand. We were introduced, and at the end of the meeting, a young Christian Thai man called Chayne came to us. He said God had given him a scripture for us. He wrote it on a piece of paper, we looked down and read Isaiah 41:10!

Through both the man at our church in New Zealand and Chayne as we arrived in Thailand, God gave us the same scripture to encourage us. And it greatly encouraged us, as our finances were very shaky at the time.

6) *I must tune into God's plan*

Paul wrote, 'God who began a good work in you will carry it on to completion.' (Phil 1:6)

When we tune into God's plan for our calling, we know He will bring it to completion. God doesn't leave His work uncompleted; He has started a work in our lives and will finish it.

If we are called to ministry (missionary, pastoral, worship leading, whatever), HE will equip us, then give us an opportunity to serve. If God calls you, He will equip you with the gift(s), the power and the authority to enable you to fulfil your call. God gives us the power to accomplish the call. And He gives us the opportunity to serve, to apply what we have learnt or seen. We must put into practice the theory. God will give us the opportunity to apply our calling, but we have to grasp that opportunity and step out in faith.

There are times when the stirring of a call is bubbling away in our hearts, and we need to respond. We need to acknowledge what God is doing. We need to say, 'I hear you, Lord. Here am I, send me.' We may not fully understand what it all means or where it might lead, but we are willing.

Are you willing to DO or GO wherever Jesus tells you?

Maybe He has work for you in Northeast Thailand. Or maybe He wants you to pray and be an intercessor for Thailand. Maybe He wants you to support those who have gone or will go in the future. Will you say, 'Here am I, send me?' Will you give Jesus permission to 'help himself to your life?' Say yes! And allow the Lord to lead you into a lifetime adventure of discovering God's tailor-made calling for your life.

Recommended Reading

The Acts of the Apostles in the New Testament was inspirational scripture for us, and we frequently found ideas there that influenced the way our ministry developed. We also found other books written by missionaries very helpful. God frequently encouraged us through the recorded lives and experiences of those other missionaries. Here are some books we recommend:

Eternity in their Hearts by Don Richardson. As mentioned in Chapter 7.

The Peace Child by Don Richardson. Reaching a Papua New Guinea tribe.

Hudson Taylor's Spiritual Secret by Howard Taylor. China ministry in the late 1800s.

To the Golden Shore: The Life of Adoniram Judson by Courtney Anderson. Pioneer work in Buddhist Burma.

Anointed for Burial by Todd and De Ann Burke. Reaching Buddhists in Cambodia in the 1970s.

Bruchko by Bruce Olson. Tribal groups in Colombia.

Death of a Guru by Rabi Maharaj. Hinduism.

www.ingramcontent.com/pod-product-compliance
Lightning Source LLC
Chambersburg PA
CBHW051450290426
44109CB00016B/1692